Doing the
Rights Thing

The authors

Maxine Molyneux has written extensively in the fields of political sociology, gender and development studies. Her most recent books are *Women's Movements in International Perspective* (2000) and three co-edited collections: *Gender and the Politics of Rights and Democracy in Latin America*, with Nikki Craske (2002); *Hidden Histories of Gender and the State in Latin America*, with Elizabeth Dore (2000); and *Gender, Justice Development and Rights*, with Shahra Razavi (2002). She has acted as consultant to a range of international agencies.

Sian Lazar was awarded a PhD in Anthropology from Goldsmiths College, University of London, in 2003. Her research was on Bolivia and resulted in an ethnography of rural-urban migrants' citizenship. She also has a Masters in Latin American Studies from the Institute of Latin American Studies, London, and has worked as a researcher for the human rights NGO, Rights and Humanity. In January 2003 she joined the Centre of Latin American Studies at Cambridge University as a researcher.

Doing the Rights Thing

Rights-based Development and Latin American NGOs

Maxine Molyneux
Sian Lazar

ITDG
PUBLISHING

Published by ITDG Publishing
103–105 Southampton Row, London WC1B 4HL, UK
www.itdgpublishing.org.uk

First published in 2003

ISBN 1 85339 568 4

A catalogue record for this book is available from the British Library.

The authors have asserted their rights under the Copyright Designs and
Patents Act 1998 to be identified as authors of this work.

ITDG Publishing is the publishing arm of the Intermediate Technology
Development Group. Our mission is to build the skills and capacity of
people in developing countries through the dissemination of information in
all forms, enabling them to improve the quality of their lives and that of
future generations.

Front cover photograph credit: Helen Shears
(originally published in *La Boletina*, Puntos de Encuentro, Nicaragua).
Shows a women's march to present their 'women's platform'
before the elections, 24 September 2000.

Typeset by The Studio Publishing Services Ltd, Exeter
Printed in Great Britain by Antony Rowe Ltd, Wiltshire

Contents

Acknowledgements

This book is based on research funded by the Department for International Development, which provided most of the funding for the fieldwork and for the publication of this book. There were many people involved in the development of this project, and we are grateful to all of them. It would be impossible to acknowledge everyone by name, but we would particularly like to thank, for their assistance in Latin America: the Antezana family, Arturo Argueta, Christina Bubba, Ricardo Calla, David Campfens, Inneke Dibbits, Olivia Harris, Javier Medina and all at Gregoria Apaza (in Bolivia); Cecilia Olea, Grecia Rojas and family, and Gina Vargas (in Peru); all at Puntos, particularly Amy Bank, Veronica Campanile, Ana Criquillon, Teresa and Wilma (in Nicaragua); Paloma Bonfil, Frine Lopez, Margarita Velazquez, the Hotel Tazelotsin, Doña Juana, Doña Victoria, Doña Esperanza, and the other Maseuals (in Mexico). We would also like to thank all those who generously gave their time to be interviewed. We would like to stress that, although all informants fully consented to the use of a tape recorder, and to the use of their views in our research, they were on the whole speaking in a personal capacity and not as official representatives of their organizations.

In England, we would like to acknowledge the input of all those who attended our consultative meetings, and thank specifically those who helped with contacts for these, provision of material and with various queries along the way: Georgina Ashworth (CHANGE), Bill Bell (SCF), Agnes Callimard (Amnesty International), Thalia Kidder (Oxfam), Karen Newman (IPPF), Sue Smith (Oxfam), Ines Smyth (Oxfam) and Kate Young. Thanks also to Sarah Bradshaw for information on Nicaragua. The authors would also like to acknowledge their gratitude to Tony Bell, formerly at the Institute of Latin American Studies, who managed the financial side of the research. Thanks too to Natalia Sobrevilla for her translations, and Paola Evans for transcription of the key in-depth interviews. David Hardcastle helped design and build the database.

Both authors thank their respective academic institutions (ILAS and Goldsmiths) for moral and material support over the course of this work. And last, but by no means least, we would like to thank Helen Marsden and an anonymous reader at ITDG Publishing for their positive and helpful comments on our manuscript.

The UK Department for International Development (DFID) supports policies, programmes and projects to promote international development. DFID provided funds for this study as part of that objective, but the views and opinions expressed are those of the authors alone.

List of figures, tables and boxes

Acronyms and abbreviations

CADEM	Centro de Asesoría y Desarrollo Entre Mujeres, Centre for Facilitation and Development between Women (Mexican NGO)
CEDAW	Convention on the Elimination of All Forms of Discrimination Against Women
CEPAL/ECLAC	Comisión Económica para América Latina y el Caribe, Economic Commission for Latin America and the Caribbean
CIDEM	Centro de Información y Desarrollo de la Mujer, Centre for Women's Information and Development (Bolivian NGO)
CSO	civil society organization
DEMUS	Estudio para la Defensa de los Derechos de la Mujer, Study for the Defense of Women's Rights (Peruvian NGO)
DFID	Department for International Development
Flora Tristan	Centro de Mujer Flora Tristan, Flora Tristan Women's Centre (Peruvian NGO)
FOVIDA	Fomento de la Vida, Encouraging Life (Peruvian NGO)
FSLN	Frente Sandinista de Liberación Nacional, National Sandinista Liberation Front
GIN	Grupo de Iniciativa Nacional del Niño y de la Niña, Children's Initiative Group (Peruvian NGO)
Gregoria Apaza, the Gregorias Women	Centro de Promoción de la Mujer Gregoria Apaza, Gregoria Apaza Centre for the Promotion of (Bolivian NGO)
GRO	grass-roots organization

HDI	Human Development Index
HIPC II	Heavily Indebted Poor Countries initiative II
ILO	International Labour Organization
ISLI	Instituto de Servicios Legales e Investigación Jurídica, Institute for Legal Services and Juridical Investigation (Bolivian NGO)
LPP	Ley de Participación Popular, Popular Participation Law
Manuela Ramos	El Movimiento Manuela Ramos, The Manuela Ramos Movement (Peruvian NGO)
MM	Maseualsiuamej Mosenyolchikuanij, Indigenous women who work together and help each other (Mexican GRO)
NGO	non-governmental organization
ODI	Overseas Development Institute
OECD	Organization for Economic Cooperation and Development
PAN	Partido de Acción Nacional, Party of National Action (Mexico)
POA	Plan Operativo Anual, Annual Operational Plan (Bolivia)
PRA	participatory rural appraisal
PRD	Partido Revolucionario Democrático, Democratic Revolutionary Party (México)
PRI	Partido Revolucionario Institucional, Institutional Revolutionary Party (México)
Puntos, Puntos de Encuentro	Puntos de Encuentro para transformar la vida cotidiana, Meeting Points for the transformation of daily life (Nicaraguan NGO)
SERPAJ	Servicio Paz y Justicia, Peace and Justice Service (Nicaraguan NGO)
TAHIPAMU	Taller de Historia y Participación de la Mujer, Workshop for the History and Participation of Women (Bolivia)

UDHR	Universal Declaration of Human Rights
UNAIDS	Joint United Nations Programme on HIV/AIDS
UNDP	United Nations Development Programme
UNFPA	United Nations Population Fund
UNHCHR	United Nations High Commission for Human Rights
UNHCR	United Nations High Commission for Refugees
UNICEF	United Nations Children Fund
UNIFEM	United Nations Development Fund for Women
VAW	violence against women
WHO	World Health Organization

Introduction

IN THE 1990s, in one of those shifts that characterize development priorities, democracy and human rights moved up the international development agenda. While in theory the link between development, democracy and rights was established in the first UN World Conference on Human Rights in 1968, it was only with the end of the Cold War that development agencies, social movements and non-governmental organizations (NGOs) began to think of new and more explicit ways to integrate democratic principles into development practice. In Latin America in particular, projects and programmes were being developed at this time to help consolidate the fragile democracies that were emerging in the aftermath of authoritarian regimes, and issues of rights, justice and good governance acquired a special significance in such contexts. In the late 1990s, the term 'rights-based development' was coined to describe these efforts, as agencies set about creating a common understanding of what rights-based priorities entailed for their practice, with the various departments of the United Nations (UN) and international NGOs taking the lead.

The revitalization of a discourse of rights was accompanied by changes in international humanitarian law and by a plethora of new agreements and conventions issuing from the UN summits that took place during the 1990s. In signing up to these, governments committed themselves to implementing changes in their laws and institutions and came under pressure from civil organizations to comply. As a result, a significant number of signatory governments to CEDAW (Convention on the Elimination of All Forms of Discrimination Against Women) reformed outdated laws which sanctioned violence against women and adopted policies to provide women with more protection.

This renewed emphasis on human rights has its supporters and opponents in all regions of the world. It has been welcomed by many who suffered and continue to suffer under authoritarian regimes, as well as by those who see it as representing the only utopian and global ideal to survive the collapse of a discredited state socialism. It is, however, also contested on a variety of grounds – political, philosophical and practical. Some governments, including a group of countries in the Muslim world and in parts of Southeast Asia, see certain elements of human rights legislation as a Western imposition, an instrument of moral imperialism or simply as representing an alien value system. The United States, too, despite its general endorsement of liberal principles, nonetheless opposes the adoption of some key elements in human rights legislation (notably the banning of the death penalty) and has refused to sign up to CEDAW or to ratify the UN Convention on the Rights of the Child. Some critics also charge that human rights legislation provides the means to violate state sovereignty – an issue posed in the wake of greater human rights intervention by the West which has been seen as inconsistent where not counterproductive. For others, rights are associated with a trend towards greater individualism, threatening the basis of collectivist or solidaristic identities and communities. Development practitioners are among those who accuse rights of being empty rhetoric, of diverting attention from more serious issues such as basic needs, poverty and economic growth. This last argument acquires particular force in contexts where macroeconomic policies and disabling debt repayments are widely perceived as disempowering the least advantaged members of society by depriving them of jobs and incomes, and undermining their access to health and education.

These are important and complex issues, each of which requires careful and informed debate. Yet however much they complicate questions of rights and democracy, they do not invalidate the appeal of the principles on which they rest. Nor do they erase the history of struggle in pursuit of them by those who have been denied rights and recognition. Whatever the origins of these principles (and the West cannot claim exclusive ownership of justice), however cynically supported at times, the language of rights and democracy has come to acquire an existence as a popular aspiration both beyond the West and outside the formal juridical and international arenas with which it is associated. These ideas have been owned both as a language and as an aspiration by a wide range of social movements for over two centuries, including women's movements, indigenous movements, and those who struggled against apartheid, slavery, caste and racism. In more recent times, international law under the auspices of the UN has increasingly embodied these principles and countless social movements have been quick to take advantage of this legislation to advance their own struggles for justice.

Yet the rights embodied in UN conventions and declarations often seem remote from the daily lives of those who most stand to benefit from it, namely the excluded and the poor. Governments sign up to conventions, agreeing in principle to respect a host of social, economic and political conditions, but often do little to observe them. Much of the population may be unaware of their rights, and even if they are aware of them they are far from being able to attain them. In recent decades, however, this distance between international instruments and local populations' awareness of their import has been narrowing. There now exists a greater range of mediations that serve to link the two. More communication through the visual and print media, greater levels of literacy and new networking possibilities offered by the Internet have all played a part in bridging the gap. However, civil society organizations (CSOs), and NGOs must also take much of the credit. They have lobbied governments to respect their commitments, they have worked closely with social movements to advance programmes of reform, and they have taken rights discourses into communities and into homes where they are debated, discussed and acted upon. Organizations and movements that work to promote an awareness of rights among disadvantaged groups are not only active in different arenas, but in this work they are involved in a process of translation, whereby apparently remote and sometimes abstract rights are 'brought down to ground level' and are made meaningful within specific national and local contexts. At the same time, those who lack power and influence have some chance of seeing their concerns conveyed upwards through the power structure – if the organizations they work with are genuinely accountable to them. Far from remaining remote and abstract, rights work more often than not implies working at and through several levels – from the micro-level to international conferences where NGOs have representation, to engaging with national states and their legal apparatuses and debating social policy and resource allocation. In these ways, the aspirations of local communities can be aligned with international agreements and used to exert pressure on states to reform their policies and improve their provision.

Beyond the evident ethical rationale and historical appeal of rights and democracy, it is also argued that together they make an essential contribution to development. At the World Social Development Summit in Copenhagen in 1986, the Declaration of the Right to Development was reaffirmed stating:

> The right to development is an inalienable human right by virtue of which every human person . . . [is] entitled to participate in, contribute to, and enjoy economic, social cultural and political development, in which all human rights and fundamental freedoms can be fully realised.

The linking of development and social integration emphasized the importance of participation, understood in the broadest sense: participation in society, in the economy and in the political life of nation states. This in turn implied empowering the excluded and the poor to enable them to participate in the development process, and creating the institutions that promote participation. In a summary of the 2002 Human Development Report, the UNDP argues that:

> . . . politics matter for human development. Reducing poverty depends as much on whether poor people have political power as on their opportunities for economic progress. Democracy has proven to be the system of governance most capable of mediating and preventing conflict and sustaining well-being. By expanding people's choices about how and by whom they are governed, democracy brings principles of participation and accountability to the process of human development.
>
> (UNDP, 2002)

If economic growth depends on, and is enhanced by, social and human development, then the quality of education and health available to a population is as important as meeting basic human needs such as housing and nutrition. As developed in the 'capabilities' approach initially conceptualized by Amartya Sen (1992), human development entails both rights and entitlements, which, if they are to be meaningful, presuppose a state of law to guarantee them. Where governments fail to secure basic social development for their populations, their countries generally also fail to compete on the global market. If a large sector of the population is unable to participate in the economy through poverty and social deprivation, their potential is denied and the economy as a whole suffers. Human development is a *sine qua non* of economic growth, and it follows that enhancing the capabilities of the poor and their realm of freedom and choice is a development priority. To be meaningful, such principles must be grounded in a conception of rights that strengthens the capacity of citizens to make legitimate claims of government. These ideas underlie some of the thinking associated with rights-based development.

Despite the continuing debate and discussion that surrounds the linking of rights to development, and the extensive literature that development agencies have produced on the subject, there is still remarkably little understanding of what rights-based development means in practice. We know little about the ways in which NGOs have worked with rights, and less about the specific regional or local understandings about rights that inform project design and implementation. Few regional analyses, let alone large-scale comparative studies, as yet exist on the different local applications of rights approaches. It is fair to say that many development agencies remain unsure of their terms of reference, priorities, evaluative criteria or conceptual definitions in regard to projects conceived within this framework.

This book was written to help fill this gap and with three aims in mind:

- to report from one region, Latin America, on the ways in which ideas drawn from the rights-based development agenda were being interpreted and applied by small-scale development agencies
- to contribute to comparative research and ongoing debate on this question
- to help clarify the meaning given by practitioners to some key terms deployed in this area of development policy.

In the chapters that follow we hear how NGO practitioners themselves not only apply these approaches, but how they position themselves in regard to some of the criticisms of rights approaches noted earlier. It is a central argument of this book that the language of rights, while internationalized and understood to have universal appeal, has specific regional resonance (see also Wilson, 1997; Cowan et al., 2001). This is strikingly evident in the Latin American case, as we will see.

Defining rights-based work

While the main question explored here is how rights were being assimilated into development practice in Latin America, the NGOs we chose to focus on were working within the broad remit of how to promote equitable development and tackle poverty. This accorded not only with our own concerns but with the priority assigned to tackling poverty and exclusion by international development agencies and the Organization for Economic Cooperation and Development (OECD) governments through their pledge to meet the International Development Targets of 2015. NGOs that prioritized the needs and rights of women and indigenous people, acknowledged to be among the poorest groups, were consequently selected for this study.

An initial assumption guiding the research was that a shift in the conceptual language and priorities of many NGOs had occurred from the late 1980s, the distinguishing elements of which were either derived from, or were in coincidence with, a new international policy consensus outlined briefly above. This shift was, of course, neither complete nor irreversible, but however partial or temporary it proves to be, there was nonetheless a discernible change in the language and practice of NGOs and other development agencies in this period.[1] The identifiable components of this transformation were: first, the adoption of strategies and discourses concerned with rights, including in the latter case a promotion of the idea of citizenship; and second, a commitment to democratic practices both within development agencies and in their relationships with those with whom they worked. We were therefore interested in NGOs that, in one way or another, expressed these two core commitments, and which were considered both innovatory and influential in their own countries and among donor communities.

A review of the policy documents of a range of large international NGOs and consultations with their representatives confirmed that a conceptual shift in NGOs' definitions of their priorities had occurred or was under way. This was expressed as a move away from an identification of their work as needs-based and service-driven to a more *strategic* approach, in which rights issues were increasingly incorporated into their work and were given special relevance in work that targeted poverty. However, this shift was not always clearly defined and in practice there were significant continuities with some prior commitments. Moreover, while there was acceptance of the general principles of human rights in development practice, some NGOs were more concerned with applying these principles to *internal* organization than in explicitly pursuing rights-based strategies as a central component of their work. Given the variability in responses to what was acknowledged to be a 'new development agenda', our choice of NGOs was governed by a broad definition of what was understood as 'rights-based work' or a 'rights-based approach'. This definition was considered relevant not only to those with an explicit human rights focus, but incorporated citizenship rights, and indigenous, children's and women's rights, precisely in order to explore the broad range of rights-based strategies that can be deployed. The working definition we developed in the course of our investigation was as follows.

Rights-based work implies that some or all of the following elements be present:

- An explicit analysis of NGO work in terms of rights.
- Advocacy and/or work with the ultimate objective of genuine participation of the target population in formal and informal decision-making processes throughout society.
- An emphasis on empowerment.

- A focus on democracy, which involved not only an engagement in some way with governmental processes at international, national or local level, but also included internal democracy and a participatory relationship with users.
- Sensitivity to issues of difference, most common being those of gender, culture, ethnicity, religion and age.
- A shift from a focus mainly on service provision to a greater emphasis on advocacy and a strategic analysis of the project's work – the aim being to change society at large as well as to improve the lives of the project users.

Rights and poverty elimination: Latin American innovations

The philosophical and moral strength of human rights lies in their universalist principles: all humans have certain rights by virtue of being born. However, it is widely acknowledged that economic disadvantage correlates with other forms of deprivation, including access to rights and justice. Structural inequalities determine wide disparities in the effective capacity to exercise rights, ones that correspond to social divisions based on class, gender, ethnicity, age, sexuality and disability. As noted, the NGOs that participated in this study worked mainly with poor women and indigenous people, both groups who suffer from the cumulative disadvantages of poverty, exclusion and discrimination. These organizations believed that tackling poverty and inequality were indissolubly linked to the capacity to bring about changes, both subjective and structural, in the conditions of the disadvantaged. They were committed to developing ways of working commensurate with this view and were developing a distinctive, and in many ways an innovative, approach to development.

A fundamental aim of their work among the poor and marginal was to promote self-respect and self-realization. This was achieved through a discourse of dignity and rights that connected ideas of a common humanity to notions of empowerment and independent agency. In Latin America this is usually defined as 'autonomy'. For the regional UN Agency, CEPAL, autonomy is 'a means of evaluating achievements in the processes of empowerment and of overcoming social exclusion. The degree to which women are capable of deciding, autonomously, their participation in the market and politics, or in civil life, is essential in order to evaluate any achievements in gender equality'.[2] Empowerment in this context is understood as the awareness that one is a subject of rights with a capacity to *act on the world* – for changes that benefit both individuals and collectivities as well as being of benefit to society as a whole.[3] In post-authoritarian Latin America, these ideas were directly linked to citizenship and democracy, understood as positive values in themselves, whether practised within the family or within the wider society and its political institutions. NGOs working within this remit sought to promote a knowledge of rights together with a range of skills, including income-generating skills, but also training in leadership and negotiation, designed to enable low-income and excluded groups to achieve voice and presence within the wider political and social world. Workshops and training sessions were therefore seen as more than the transference of skills and knowledge, and became a shared, collective experience. Participants often recollected them in emotional terms as having 'changed their lives', 'started them on a new journey' or 'opened their eyes'. This sense of personal transformation, even more than any new knowledge gained, particularly stirred them. If horizons were extended, and individual worth and dignity were valued, for many it was also the trust and solidarity that the group created through sharing histories, difficulties or goals that gave them strength, self-confidence and the inspiration to reinvent themselves as active, autonomous subjects in their communities, family and societies.[4]

Finding a voice, retrieving agency, and overcoming the isolation and powerlessness that is the lot of many, especially low-income women and indigenous people, were not merely by-products of the learning process but were an integral part of it, necessary to the fulfilment of the broader goals of the project. These goals could at times seem diffuse, even remote: promoting citizenship and democracy, tackling social exclusion, empowering the poor. Nonetheless, NGOs committed to rights work not only considered such goals valid in themselves, but also *unrealizable* without subjective microtransformations of this kind. There were also potential multiplier effects of such transformations, in the form of new networks being built, role models being created and positive values being disseminated. Moreover, as individuals interacted with their kin or colleagues in new ways which implied exercising certain rights – the right to be treated properly, the right to act autonomously, the right to be free of violence and to speak their mind – they also affirmed new norms in their behaviour and practice. Prior to attending such workshops, many women reported that even if they aspired to such rights, they seemed unrealizable in a context where a husband's permission to attend meetings, to travel, to work, to use contraception or to voice an opinion was often denied, and the penalty for disobeying could be physical punishment, even divorce (see Townsend et al., 1999). Self-realization therefore was closely linked to rights in this perspective; if women and other disadvantaged groups were to be full participants in the development process and in the consolidation of democracy, their rights, needs and capacities had to be recognized. This was a core dimension of 'people-centred development'.

The elements of this approach and the working assumptions of those who worked to develop it can be summarized as follows:

- **Favourable opportunity context:** governments' adoption of international legislation on human rights had provided new mechanisms through which campaigning NGOs could pressurize governments for legislative and policy change in favour of disadvantaged groups such as women. At the same time, governments who signed up to these new legal instruments had a duty to respect them and became vulnerable to criticism if they did not.
- **Macro–micro linkages:** human rights legislation had implications at the microsocial interpersonal level; for example, families had to respect the rights of their members, and specific bodies of legislation such as CEDAW enabled women to demand that husbands and fathers respect their right to live without violence. Even if not encoded into national law, such rights could be used to challenge traditional prerogatives and practices. This implied a transformation of *personal* values.
- **Changing mentalities:** this transformation means respecting the dignity of those who express their needs or make claims in terms of rights: no longer asking for favours, claimants become subjects with rights and entitlements. On a personal level, this realization alone can be empowering, and enhance self-esteem and well-being.
- **Empowerment:** a key concept in the lexicon of rights work, signifying at once self-realization and the perception of oneself as a subject of rights, with a capacity to act on the world and change it.
- **Participation:** a fundamental principle of NGO practice, which displaced top-down decision making with more horizontal and democratic flows of demand making and needs satisfaction. Such demand making and the satisfaction of those demands is the means by which rights are exercised. For example, women and young people can collectively demand that their communities respect their right to participate in decision making; indigenous peoples can demand that their land rights be respected by the state and private enterprises.
- **Strategic action:** human rights are not only a language with which to represent demands, they are also a mechanism for thinking *strategically*. Such strategies encourage active rather than passive behaviour, and, at their best, empower the poor to analyse their

personal situation, attribute responsibility and work out the means to improve it. The formulation of demands can therefore be linked to political and policy goals, moving from the immediate local arena to the broader environment.

- **Self-defined objectives:** development objectives are also likely to be more effective in meeting the needs of the poor if they are able to acquire a voice, define their own requirements and claim them as entitlements. The poor are not, however, a unified category, and such objectives must be defined in accordance with the needs of different groups in poverty.

- **Sustainability:** such approaches should contribute to sustainability. If people are empowered to make and define their own demands of the appropriate institutions (governmental, community and familial), and the mechanisms for them to do so are in place, they are more likely to be effective and less reliant on mediators, who may not always be there, or be willing to collaborate.

Rights-based strategies were in these various ways seen to enhance the capacity of disadvantaged groups to make their demands heard and to act in pursuit of such demands at personal, local, national and international levels. Such an approach was often contrasted with other models of development practice, notably ones which can be defined as essentially concerned with basic needs satisfaction (Streeten et al., 1981; Grindle, 1992) and which conceived of the relations between donor and recipient in terms of 'beneficiaries'. Rights-based work supposes an active, not a passive, recipient of aid, a subject of rights capable of influencing outcomes and making legitimate demands in a shared endeavour. Table 1 illustrates this contrast.

A substantial literature on the role of NGOs in development work has noted a shift in both their orientation and organisational forms over recent decades (Macdonald, 1997; Bebbington and Thiele, 1993; Edwards and Hulme, 1992). A major part of this shift has been away from paternalistic models of provision to ones that are more participatory and consultative. However, other changes can also be detected, involving the strategies adopted by NGOs with respect to their objectives and the relationships they establish with the people with whom they are working. As noted, these changes have to do crucially with ideas of partnership, where rights and citizenship replace paternalism and what is known in Latin America as *asistencialismo*, or charity. Needs too, while still centrally addressed, are reframed in terms of broader strategic visions, which encompass ideas of rights and entitlement.

The move from a limited conception of need, conceived in terms of meeting a minimum of basic requirements to a focus on rights, entails

Table 1 Differences between needs and rights in development

Needs satisfaction	Rights-based work
Beneficiaries: passive recipients of paternalistic service provision	Users: active participants, strategic planning in partnership in a shared endeavour
Clientelist relations	Citizenship relations
Needs defined from above	Rights to define and demand needs
Needs satisfaction	Empowerment with needs satisfaction
Practical interests	Links made between practical and strategic interests; emphasis on transformative practices
NGOs: based on goodwill, 'charity'	Professionalization, specialization. Institutionalization; focus on transparency, accountability and internal democracy
Donor–NGO hierarchy; NGOs asking for favours	Donor–NGO partnership

a shift towards embracing a more strategic vision of what citizens are entitled to and require for their own further development. This difference was expressed in an earlier framework for analysing women's interests, which contrasted policies associated with meeting practical needs and those which worked to advance strategic interests, where the latter entailed the achievement of broader structural changes in the distribution of power and resources. Strategic visions have in recent times been associated with ideas of rights and citizenship, and in Latin America strategic demands have been formulated in relation to projects of democratizing states and social relations (Molyneux, 1985, 2000b).

A note on the research process

The research for this book was sponsored by the UK Department for International Development (DFID) and was originally conceived as a pilot study which could be adapted and applied to a broader range of countries and different sociocultural contexts. In that sense, we saw it as aiming to generate rather than test research propositions, and we therefore designed our methodology with this in mind, to be as qualitative and flexible as possible. We carried out research in four countries in Latin America: Mexico, Peru, Nicaragua and Bolivia. These countries correspond to ones included in the project funding priorities of the

British government, and were in addition countries in which we were well placed, through specialist knowledge, experience and contacts, to work most effectively. The research began in 1998 and was completed at the end of 1999. It involved three main phases:

1   An extensive literature review and preparatory consultative process in London with development practitioners, scholars and representatives from international NGOs.
2   Participatory fieldwork combined with interviews with informants in the four countries, with a total of 13 NGOs and one grass-roots organization (GRO) investigated.
3   A final process of consultation was carried out in which the findings of the research were presented to informants, practitioners, scholars and collaborators in the field.

The methodology developed for the fieldwork, based on rapid appraisal[5] methods, combined a variety of research techniques involving qualitative methodologies, semi-structured interviews with individuals and groups, observational work and participatory methods. We chose reputational techniques to select the most innovatory NGOs working in the area of rights, and the individuals most informed about rights-based NGO activities. It was the ideas of these innovators and the range of practices possible within rights-based approaches that we were interested in, rather than statistical analysis. Our informants therefore ranged from NGO workers to associated professionals (academics, government workers). As well as interviewing those at project administration and policy levels, we interviewed some users of NGO services. A longer period was spent in Bolivia at the beginning of the fieldwork, in order to develop and further refine the interview questions and research methodologies elaborated in the UK. Throughout our research, we observed strict ethical standards, in issues such as informed consent, confidentiality and informant control over the research process.

We considered the research process as reflexive and participatory, and involved our informants, whether users of NGO services, NGO workers or professionals, in consultations about the methods and findings of the research. Early drafts of the report were distributed to participating NGOs for comment, and the findings were translated into Spanish for wider discussion. The period of fieldwork included in-depth investigations of two NGOs, which are presented in Chapter 8 as case studies to illustrate the variable approaches to rights-based work found in Latin America.

While we focused on Latin America, the consultation exercises carried out with NGOs and development experts at various stages suggested that the findings were of relevance to policy makers and practitioners not only in the Latin American region but also in Africa, and South and Southeast Asia. We hope that the Latin American experience, innovatory in many ways, will contribute to a fuller understanding of the practices which have evolved in response to the new approaches to development and of the potential that it offers in ongoing efforts to secure more equitable, effective, and inclusionary development outcomes.

The NGOs that participated in the research

As noted, we investigated the views and activities of 13 NGOs and one GRO in Latin America. Table 2 provides details of the organizations that collaborated with our research project. The work they undertook covered five main areas: first, and not surprisingly, most were involved in forms of service provision, entailing direct contact with members of their target group. Examples are legal services (including taking up legal cases on an individual basis), health services (which included advice centres and psychological counselling) and the provision of a broad range of capacity-building educational workshops. Such workshops typically involved the training of a network of legal trainers and facilitators to advise members of their communities on specific aspects of rights.

Of secondary but increasing importance was the provision of technical support for other, usually community-based, organizations. Such support was largely delivered by similar methods, i.e. capacity-building workshops, but also included giving advice on empowerment issues such as advocacy and legal skills required for political negotiation. A number of smaller and newer NGOs concentrated on organizational strengthening and *acompanimiento* (providing ongoing support and advice on administrative and strategic matters) for community organizations.

Third, all the NGOs were strongly committed to campaigning and lobbying work. Some used precedent-setting legal cases for this purpose, others worked through lobbying policy makers, local government officials and parliamentarians. All worked to change public opinion, using leaflets, posters, books and articles in newspapers, often resulting from their own research. This overlapped with a fourth area of work, network servicing. Of growing importance in the 1990s, this involved coordination between NGOs and national governments, promoted the provision of capacity-building workshops to network members on a range of different issues, and offered a means of collaborating for the purposes of collective campaigning.

Finally, a key activity that fed into all other areas of work for many of the organizations in our study was research. Independent, high-quality scholarly research on 'target populations' was seen as not only of practical value (to facilitate campaigning or enable more effective direct work), but also as indispensable for ethical reasons. Feminist and other scholars have criticized the monopoly held by Northern academics of representations of the South (Mohanty, 1991a,b). Many Latin American feminist NGOs have, from their beginnings, seen part of their agenda as redressing this imbalance through the production of a local knowledge base, although most complained that there was a severe shortage of funding for this purpose.

It should be emphasized that no NGO discussed here falls squarely into one or other of these categories of work. However, a trend that would bear more study is the distinction between *direct* service provision to target populations and *indirect* service provision, where the users are other NGOs or community organizations. While it is generally recognized that civil society is of critical importance for rights-based approaches to development, there is a gap in our understanding of the practical ways in which what Moser et al. (2001: 45) term 'effective pro-poor advocacy institutions' have functioned. This book begins to address that gap, as we found that several organizations had developed in the past 15 years with the primary focus of providing technical support for other organizations, even though they are *not* network coordinators – a longer-established mechanism for the provision of this type of non-direct service. The older NGOs in our study, with over 15 years of experience, tended to be more involved in direct service provision, although many were beginning to diversify into activities closely associated with technical support. These organizations also tended to be larger, and in many instances better funded than the smaller, more narrowly focused NGOs, both factors perhaps accounting for the difference in emphasis.

The exception to this general characterization is the Nicaraguan organization Puntos de Encuentro (*Puntos de Encuentro para Transformar la Vida Cotidiana*, Meeting Points for the Transformation of Daily Life, henceforth Puntos). Although relatively new (10 years old), the organization was large and, at the time of the research, well funded,[6] yet focused its activities on non-direct, non-service-driven areas: technical support for other organizations, coordination activities (without being a network) and campaigning. It is for this reason that Puntos provides a good case study (see Chapter 8). The other case study, in Mexico, was specifically concerned to highlight the link between a GRO and a recently established small NGO that provides organizations in the region with technical support.

This trend of newer, non-direct NGOs may help to enhance the capacity of those most in need to define and pursue what they demand of resource providers (particularly the state, but increasingly including international donors: multilateral, bilateral and Northern NGOs). However, it is also a product (and possibly a motor) of the proliferation of NGOs in Latin America, and represents yet another administrative layer between the people the project is designed to reach and those with resources to distribute. This mediating layer is composed largely of middle class professionals with a high level of education, many of whom would, in times past, have worked for the state. The implications of such a development for the political participation and/or the empowerment of low-income groups have yet to be worked through.

Structure of the book

The first two chapters of this book provide the background to the emergence and application of rights-based development. The remaining chapters discuss the ways in which Latin American NGOs have worked with rights. Chapter 1 examines the recent origins of rights-based development work in the liberal internationalist agenda of the 1990s and discusses some of the ways that international development agencies such as the UN and the World Bank have absorbed rights into their programmes. Chapter 2 provides a brief overview of the Latin American context and of the four countries in which the research was carried out. It emphasizes how different rights-based strategies interact and are seen by practitioners in determinate contexts.

Chapter 3 discusses the changes in priorities and practice as experienced by NGOs in Latin America, exploring their views on the 'new' concepts of rights and citizenship and the interactions between rights and needs in NGOs' conceptions of their day-to-day work. Chapter 4 examines some of the activities that NGOs consider to be part of their rights-based approaches to development, linking them to ideas of participation and empowerment. Chapter 5 highlights a specific example of a particularly effective rights-based campaign in Latin America – that on violence against women – and assesses the theoretical implications of the greater emphasis on issues of rights and especially citizenship. Chapter 6 then turns to examine the problems that NGOs have experienced in regard to such work. Chapter 7 moves from the conceptual to the more practical level, analysing the reconfigurations of relationships in development that have arisen from decisions to focus more on rights, and the practical implications of such shifts. It begins to assess the problems and opportunities for evaluation, relationships with donors, and relationships with beneficiaries, and what might be conceived of as good rights-based practice among NGOs. While most donor money goes to national governments, recipient governments are now more frequently looking to NGOs for input in designing their programmes, as well as for their implementation. Thus it is crucial to understand processes of rights-based approaches to development from a ground-level perspective. Chapter 8 consists of case studies of two NGOs, one in Nicaragua, the other in Mexico, which illustrate the work that is carried out in accordance with the principles defined above. The conclusions follow.

Table 2   Profiles of NGOs that took part in this study

Centro de Mujer Flora Tristan (Peru)	
Type*	Network coordinator, **service provision (legal, educational, health)**, ‡ technical support for other organizations, academic research
Beneficiaries*†	**Women**, young people
Type of work	Educational workshops, individual consultations, public awareness campaigns, organizational strengthening, coordination, research, lobby
Main themes*	Rights

Centro de Promoción de la Mujer Gregoria Apaza (Bolivia)	
Type*	Network coordinator, **service provision (legal, educational)**
Beneficiaries*†	**Women**, young people
Type of work	Educational workshops, group and individual consultations, public awareness campaigns, organizational strengthening, coordination, research, lobby
Main themes*	Gender

CIDEM (Bolivia)	
Type*	Network coordinator, **service provision (legal, educational, health)**, academic research
Beneficiaries*†	Women
Type of work	Educational workshops, group and individual consultations, public awareness campaigns, organizational strengthening, lobby
Main themes*	Rights, gender, citizenship

(continued)

Table 2 (continued)

Colectivo Gaviota (Nicaragua)

Type*	**Service provision (educational)**, academic research
Beneficiaries*†	Women
Type of work	Educational workshops, public awareness campaigns, organizational strengthening, research
Main themes*	Gender, rights, human rights of women

DEMUS (Peru)

Type*	**Service provision (legal)**, academic research
Beneficiaries*†	Women
Type of work	Individual consultations, public awareness campaigns, research, lobby
Main themes*	Rights

Fomento de la Vida (FOVIDA) (Peru)

Type*	**Service provision (educational)**, technical support for other organizations
Beneficiaries*†	Women
Type of work	Educational workshops, organizational strengthening
Main themes*	Gender, leadership

Grupo de Iniciativa Nacional del Niño y de la Niña (GIN) (Peru)

Type*	**Network coordinator**, service provision (legal), technical support for other organizations
Beneficiaries*†	Young people
Type of work	Educational workshops, public awareness campaigns, research, lobby
Main themes*	Rights

ISLI (Bolivia)

Type*	Service provision (legal), **technical support for other organizations**
Beneficiaries*	Indigenous people
Type of work	Educational workshops, individual consultations, organizational strengthening, coordination
Main themes*	Rights/law

Manuela Ramos (Peru)

Type*	**Service provision (legal, educational, health)**, technical support for other organizations, academic research
Beneficiaries*†	Women, young people
Type of work	Educational workshops, individual consultations, public awareness campaigns, organizational strengthening, coordination, research, lobby
Main themes*	Rights

(continued)

Table 2   (continued)

Puntos de Encuentro (Nicaragua)

Type*	Network coordinator, service provision (educational), **technical support for other organizations**
Beneficiaries* †	Women, young people
Type of work	Educational workshops, public awareness campaigns, organizational strengthening, coordination, research, lobby
Main themes*	Autonomy

Servicio Paz y Justicia (SERPAJ) (Nicaragua)

Type*	**Service provision (educational)**
Beneficiaries* †	General
Type of work	Educational workshops, public awareness campaigns, organizational strengthening
Main themes*	Peace, justice

TAHIPAMU (Bolivia)

Type*	**Technical support for other organizations**, academic research
Beneficiaries* †	Women
Type of work	Educational workshops, public awareness campaigns, organizational strengthening, coordination, research, lobby
Main themes*	Rights

TAREA (Peru)

Type*	**Service provision (educational)**, academic research
Beneficiaries* †	Young people
Type of work	Educational workshops, public awareness campaigns, organizational strengthening, coordination, research, lobby
Main themes*	Education

---

* Main themes and priority activities (shown in bold type) indicate the authors' view.

† All said that they were working for poor and/or marginalized sectors of the population.

‡ Service provision defined as direct contact with individuals from beneficiary population – can be legal, i.e. taking up cases, educational/training, health, including psychological. This table distinguishes between educational, legal and other.

Table 3   Profiles of organizations in the case studies

Maseualsiuamej Mosenyolchikuanij (Mexico)	
Type*	**GRO – income generation**, service provision (educational)
Beneficiaries*†	Indigenous women
Type of work	Collective marketing, educational workshops, coordination
Main themes*	Poverty

Centro de Asesoría y Desarrollo Entre Mujeres (CADEM) (Mexico)	
Type*	**Technical support for other organizations**, service provision (educational), academic research
Beneficiaries*†	Indigenous women
Type of work	Educational workshops, public awareness campaigns, organizational strengthening, coordination, research
Main themes*	Rights

* Main themes and priority activities (shown in bold type) indicate the authors' view.

† All said that they were working for poor and/or marginalized sectors of the population.

1 Rights in development: conceptual issues

RIGHTS-BASED DEVELOPMENT as it evolved in the 1990s was a product of a specific historical moment, one that was quite exceptional politically. The end of the Cold War signalled a renewed confidence in liberal values, confirmed by the restoration of democratic governments in Latin America and the former Soviet Union, and the end of apartheid in South Africa. At the end of the decade, all but a handful of nations were ruled by governments that claimed to be democracies, while the international human rights movement was revitalized by the 1993 UN Conference on Human Rights in Vienna. At the same time, the major international development institutions turned their attention to poverty alleviation and to promoting good governance, understood as efficient, accountable administration in both government and non-government institutions. This entailed substantial political and legal reform, and a spate of new constitutions resulted, notably in South Africa and Latin America.

These different elements combined to forge a new consensus in policy arenas over the importance of integrating issues of rights and democracy into development practice. Along with the greater commitment to tackling poverty, rights-based development led, among other things, to an emphasis being placed on participatory methods and on bottom-up development, both as a more democratic way of managing projects and in order to avoid the pitfalls of development practice imposed from above.

The neoliberal policy failures of the 1980s renewed concerns over poverty and the high social costs of many stabilization and adjustment packages, particularly in the former Soviet Union, Latin America and sub-Saharan Africa. Global inequalities rose sharply in the last decades of the twentieth century while poverty remained a persistent and, in some countries, a growing phenomenon. Growing criticism of the policies of international development institutions was one reason why the 1990s were marked by a partial retreat from 'market fundamentalism', while there were renewed attempts to rethink development policy. The turn to an explicit focus on poverty alleviation, endorsed by the World Bank from the late 1980s, was a central plank of the 'post-adjustment' development agenda. However, whereas poverty had been addressed in the 1970s through more universal welfare principles and an emphasis on 'meeting basic needs', in the 1990s the approach was to target the most needy, with a rhetorical emphasis on empowering the poor and securing their rights and participation (Streeten et al., 1981; Caulfield, 1997; Sano, 2000; World Bank, 2001). These policies converged with the 'good governance' agenda in a number of interesting ways. For many development agencies, good governance meant creating a regulatory context that allowed economic stability and increased foreign investment. In turn, this implied a recognition that institutional inefficiency and its common correlate, corruption, was creating a crisis of legitimacy, inhibiting development and obstructing efforts to alleviate poverty. As the DFID White Paper expressed it:

> Efforts to reduce poverty are often undermined by bribery and corruption. . . . It is generally poor people who bear the heaviest cost of corrupt activities. If people are to be able to exercise their rights and live in a just society, countries must have a framework of law and regulation. To this end, we will support reforms in the legal sector and help make governments and the civil service work more efficiently (DFID, 1997: 16).

For success in these areas, sounder institutional management with appropriate transparency and accountability was required. However, implicit too was a predisposition in favour of democratic governance along with free market economics, although in practice the former was increasingly diluted or waived under pressure from some governments on either liberal or conservative grounds.

While good governance agendas have been subject to criticism on a variety of grounds (Bøås, 1998; Donnelly, 1999; Evans, 2000), it is arguable that they were important precursors to, and allies of, human rights agendas in development, particularly from the perspective of donor agencies. Good governance policies were a means by which donor governments in the West have linked their advocacy of civil and political rights to that of economic growth in arguing that the stability required for the latter can only come via democratic political systems. Bilateral and multilateral agencies are well placed through conditionalities to require strengthening the institutionalization of partner governments, who may also see advantages in terms of their own political interests. Indeed, as Donnelly notes, 'There is a growing tendency to emphasize compatibilities between civil and political rights and development. For example, international financial institutions in the 1990s have increasingly emphasized the economic contributions of "good governance"' (Donnelly, 1999: 627). This focus on 'getting institutions right' strengthened as the doctrinaire market-oriented approach to development gave way at the end of the 1980s to a greater acceptance of the role of state intervention in both economic and human development. Some commentators argue that this shift, which converged with the promotion of human rights, represents a positive step towards what Hans-Otto Sano terms a more 'actor- and social-oriented order' (Sano, 2000: 741). Good governance was also understood to imply greater citizen access to the process of government, whether this be in free and fair national elections, or in local level engagement with policy processes.

The idea of incorporating rights into development therefore had many tributary currents and was promoted by a range of institutions and agents in the course of the 1990s. The corpus of international human rights legislation, along with other UN protocols, agreements and statements, established the fundamental principles and provided the overall framework for rights-based work. But much of this had been in place for 50 years or more. It was only in the post-authoritarian context of the 1990s that this work was revitalized when governments, international development agencies, social movements and NGOs combined to elaborate the connection between rights and development. The result was a proliferation of legal instruments and policy recommendations and a growing scholarly literature on the subject.

Much of this work was stimulated by and fed into the UN's end-of-millennium summits. The various departments of the UN were actively engaged in developing conceptions of rights, including the right to development, as well as in refining the meanings of social and cultural rights, indigenous, children's and women's rights. As noted, the Vienna Human Rights Conference of 1993 provided an important impetus for this work, but other summits also focused on various aspects of rights. The Cairo Conference on Population in 1994, the Social Summit in Copenhagen in 1995 and the Fourth World Conference on Women in Beijing, also in 1995, gave a high profile to the role of human rights in their proposals for action, broadening normative interpretations of human rights with their emphasis on the need to tackle inequality and exclusion as well as to design and implement appropriate social policies.

Governments, particularly the Northern Social Democratic states, also played an important role in this process. In Britain, the Labour government's reorganized Department for International Development (DFID) was one of the first governmental agencies to highlight the importance of human rights in its policy statements. The White Paper of 1997 was followed by a number of strategic policy documents that addressed the issue of how the Department should implement its rights-based agenda (DFID, 2000a,b,c).

Arguably, however, the most influential actors in promoting, and to an extent also radicalizing, rights-based agendas were international NGOs. They were able to take advantage of a change in their own circumstances to bring more leverage to bear on international policy settings and to help set and promote agendas in development work. NGOs had seen an increase in their scope for influencing policy agendas from the 1980s, not least through acquiring greater rights of participation in such agenda-setting forums as UN summits and their preparatory and follow-up meetings. This incorporation of non-state actors as observers and consultants was allowed in principle from the earliest days of the UN, but NGOs acquired considerably greater presence in recent times, notably in the end-of-millennium summits where more organizations acquired accreditation than before. Argued by some to have brought about a 'pluralization', albeit limited, of global governance, it meant that multilateral economic and policy institutions had actively to engage with non-governmental and civil society organizations and through them with their constituencies.

The expanded scope of NGO involvement was one of the most significant developments in recent decades and reflected the greater role they were playing in development processes. This was partly a result of the international political context, and was driven from the 1980s by the prevailing distrust of the state and by neoliberal policies that sought to reduce its size and limit its functions. NGOs, seen as more efficient and less corrupt than many states, took on an increasingly important role in service delivery and in the production of development knowledge. During the 1990s, NGOs debated rights agendas, and sometimes opposed them, but many were also promoters of rights discourse in international forums, as well as practitioners working with rights at project level, generating a range of innovative programmes and projects.

Throughout the 1990s, a growing number of influential Northern NGOs incorporated the language of rights into their development work (*inter alia* Oxfam, Save the Children Fund, Action Aid, International Planned Parenthood Federation). This anticipated and at the same time influenced the shifts undergone by government development agencies. In turn, NGOs were influenced by these agencies' demands on them. When seeking governmental and private funding, NGOs were increasingly impelled to orient their work strategically. They were, for example, required to justify their activities in terms of the social impact on the wider community, rather than restricting it to service provision for a narrow base of users. If this was partly driven by funding squeezes, such an emphasis was welcomed by many NGOs, who shared in the enthusiasm for the more strategic principles expressed in human rights discourses. Northern NGOs were also influenced by the concerns and activities of their Southern partners. All these factors, combined with the changes in the international political and developmental context described above, contributed to a shift in NGO priorities towards more rights-based work.

As multilateral and bilateral donor agencies, as well as the larger Northern NGOs, took up issues of rights and democracy in their development work, other, less enthusiastic agencies were prompted to respond. The World Bank, initially hesitant as its constitution commits it to political neutrality and bars it from activity deemed 'political', nonetheless became increasingly involved with the human rights issues raised by environmental protection, gender equity and civil society participation (Moser et al., 2001: 9). In 1998, on the occasion of the fiftieth anniversary of the Universal Declaration of Human Rights (UDHR), it published a report on development and human rights which stated that

> the World Bank believes that creating the conditions for the attainment of human rights is a central and irreducible goal of development. ... The world now accepts that sustainable development is impossible without human rights. What has been missing is the recognition that the advancement of an interconnected set of human rights is impossible *without development* (World Bank, 1998: 3, emphasis in original).

In its World Development Report of 2000/01, the Bank published what some saw as a landmark statement, where it stressed the importance of the 'empowerment of the poor' in attacking poverty (World Bank, 2001). The concept of empowerment had been enthusiastically taken up by NGOs in the 1980s, particularly by those working with women, and in some interpretations it was explicitly linked to rights: 'real' empowerment meant gaining rights and leverage in decision-making arenas. More recently, the Bank has begun to explore how to incorporate rights into its approach to poverty alleviation. An Overseas Development Institute (ODI) workshop held in London in June of 2001 was designed to feed into the World Bank's exploration of how to combine rights-based and sustainable livelihoods approaches in its thinking on poverty elimination (see Moser et al., 2001). In the words of a member of the Bank's general council, '. . . our mission of fighting poverty directly involves the advancement of human rights through legal and judicial reform, and tackling health, environment education and other basic needs' (Bretton Woods, 2002: 1). Other bilateral agencies, including those from Australia, Germany, Norway, Sweden, Switzerland and Denmark, responded in similar ways (Sano 2000; UNDP, 2000). Both UNDP and UNICEF developed rights-based policy agendas for their work (UNDP, 2000; Rozga, 2001; van Weerelt, 2001). In some cases this represented a new departure; in others, such as the UN Women's agency, UNIFEM, it represented a strengthening of a pre-existing agenda.

Such developments gained momentum in a favourable international political environment. As the ideological polarities of the Cold War faded, so the scope for rights work broadened. The historic divide between Western governments that prioritized civil and political rights and those who gave primacy to social and economic rights gave way to a more holistic and integral view of rights as mutually interdependent, at least at the level of rhetoric. This integral view was affirmed in the 1993 Vienna UN Conference, and in subsequent UN summits international endorsement was gained for the principle of the indivisibility of human rights. The new consensus evident in the 1995 Copenhagen UN Social Summit responded to demands from the developing countries for social provision to be understood in terms of rights and entitlements rather than being left to market forces. Hans-Otto Sano argues that 'during the 1990s, development was increasingly perceived as a right, whereas earlier it had been perceived as an instrument of solidarity' (Sano, 2000: 736). In this spirit, Amnesty International, historically a rights-based organization with a traditional focus on civil and political rights, voted in August 2001 to extend its mandate to include discrimination understood as the violation of social, economic and cultural rights (Amnesty International, 2001). However, such enthusiasm for rights was not unopposed: some developing countries viewed rights agendas as a form of Western hegemony and entered multiple reservations exempting them from compliance with certain clauses, notably where these were argued to be in conflict with religion or custom. These latter usually implicated women's rights (Charlesworth and Chinkin, 2000; Merry, 2001). Even among supporters, opinion continues to be divided on how far to apply rights to development, given that the proliferation of rights has produced problems of legal consistency, and has raised false expectations of what governments can or will deliver. A significant number of governments remain critical of universalist principles, and in some areas, notably family law, invoke multicultural arguments to defend the reservations they enter on becoming signatories (Molyneux and Razavi, 2002). Meanwhile, the focus on security issues following the attacks of September 11 2001 has set the human rights agenda back, causing some to wonder if the ascendancy of the human rights agenda is over.

Participation, empowerment and rights

If good governance, poverty relief and human rights were central components in the conceptual shift by donor agencies from needs to rights, there was another important element that made its appearance within the policy documents of the new development agenda. This was the increasing emphasis within development intervention on *participation*. Inspired by principles of user participation, development practice was to be (in theory at least) more democratic, more responsive to local needs and knowledge, and more ethical and efficient than top-down 'technocratic' development (see Nelson and Wright, 1995 for a critical overview). Participatory development was not itself a new concept and had enjoyed a certain popularity among radicals from the 1960s while also being promoted by USAID. But it acquired a new momentum and broader acceptance in the 1990s as a result of both academic knowledge production and practical evaluations and criticisms of the failures of development projects (Ferguson, 1990; Hobart, 1993; Nelson and Wright, 1995; Scott, 1998). The work of Robert Chambers (e.g. Chambers, 1997) was influential here. The Copenhagen Summit went as far as recommending that people from disadvantaged groups should be helped to participate in governmental processes and bodies (Ferguson, 1999). The focus on participation led development agencies to stress the *processes* of development, and human rights were seen by some agencies, such as UNICEF and UNDP, as both a *means* to better programmes and greater efficiency, and as an *end* in themselves.

Recent contributions to the elaboration of rights-based development from scholars and from UN and bilateral development agencies have stressed the role of rights in claim making, enabling the principles of participation, empowerment and accountability to be put into practice (DFID, 2000c; UNDP, 2000; Moser et al., 2001; Rozga, 2001). A general consensus has developed among scholars, activists and governments that conceptualizing work in terms of rights implies at least some consideration of mechanisms for framing and making claims. Latin American NGOs in this study agreed that rights-based strategies enhanced the capacity of low-income and marginal groups to make their demands heard and to act in pursuit of such demands, at local, national and international levels. However, their ideas differed from those promoted in more 'top-down' documents in their stress on the personal, subjective implications of rights and empowerment. This distinctive element in their practice draws on some earlier ideas found in liberation theology and in the work of the Brazilian popular educationalist Paolo Freire.

From this perspective, rights were approached in a less legal and institutional sense, through a focus on what Craig Scott calls the 'social meanings' of rights (Scott, 1999: 636). Although many NGOs worked within institutional frameworks, in legal literacy training or educational work, they also had a strong focus on the person as a citizen and/or subject of rights. NGO workers felt that it was particularly crucial to engender a feeling of rights ownership among those with whom they worked, attempting to infuse daily life with new meaning and different values. Creating a democratic culture and the personal attributes that would sustain it was central to this thinking in post-authoritarian Latin America. The transition to institutional democracy was itself a major challenge, but it also implied changes in the practice of citizens that would enhance the democratic character of civil society. As Sano argues, the international agencies' emphasis on good governance implies more than institutional change in the direction of liberal democracy: it also implies democratization as a 'political culture or behavioural norm' throughout society (Sano, 2000: 736). This latter meaning is taken particularly seriously in Latin America among NGOs and citizens' movements and has been the basis of a wide range of initiatives designed to transform social attitudes. Development agencies, however, have tended to place more emphasis on the institutional level, where the demand for change is urgent and the results are often more tangible. Nonetheless, in Latin America, NGOs were promoting change on more personal, subjective levels, which they considered essential for the sustainability of democracy as well as for the success of broader development interventions. A focus on empowerment was a central part of these approaches, understood not just as a matter of creating appropriate frameworks for accountability, but implying that the development of self-esteem and the self-realization of participants was essential in enhancing their capacity to act on the world. For low-income women who are often in subservient positions in the family and subject to male authority in society at large, empowerment can involve them in challenging power relations at all levels, including the most intimate. More broadly, as Moser et al. argue: 'Rights form a valuable strategic entry point for addressing the ways in which power imbalances act to deny the marginalized access to assets and opportunities necessary for a secure and sustainable livelihood' (Moser et al., 2001: 22). In a very practical sense, they also address questions of powerlessness, agency and personhood among those whom they are intended to benefit.

To claim personhood, either as citizen or as a subject of human rights more generally, is a claim to humanity; as John Gledhill points out, 'practical denial of rights can only be justified by postulating essential differences that reduce the claims to humanity of those against whom one discriminates' (Gledhill, 1997: 7). Therefore, making rights claims is a radical claim for substantive agency by various categories of person, such as 'the poor', 'poor people', women and children. A full appreciation of this is crucial if social, economic and cultural rights are to be more than simply a way of codifying and claiming needs. At government level such an awareness is seldom if ever evident, and the policies necessary to bring about such changes would require levels of political will that are rarely present.

Social and economic rights

Rights, understood as legal entitlements, serve as a way to articulate demands, but also imply the existence of certain conditions for their fulfilment. The UNDP, for example, has argued that rights frame universal claims to a set of social arrangements that protect certain entitlements and freedoms (UNDP, 2000). The UN rights framework commits governments to providing the institutional framework for such social arrangements. Yet many governments have contested these implications and have disputed the degree to which states should assume legal and financial responsibility to protect social and economic rights. If education and public health provision are understood to be matters of state responsibility, how does this square with current policy preferences for the private sector to have an increasing role in these areas? Whether rights can be enjoyed in the absence of responsibility is at the heart of this dispute. Classic legal formulations of rights recognize corresponding duty holders who have the obligation to guarantee these rights (Donnelly, 1985, 1999; Perry, 1996; Hausermann, 1998; UNDP, 2000; Moser et al., 2001); legislating rights without allocating duties make declarations meaningless, or as Jeremy Bentham said of the Rights of Man, they amount to little more than 'nonsense upon stilts'.[7] Whether rights carry obligations, and whether they can be meaningful unless they do, is therefore a central issue for advocates of social, economic and cultural rights. A statement adopted by the UN Committee of the Economic and Social Council argues that:

> Critically, rights and obligations demand accountability: unless supported by a system of accountability, they can become no more than window dressing. Accordingly, the human rights approach to poverty emphasises obligations and requires that all duty-holders, including states and international organisations, are held to account for their conduct in relation to international human rights law (United Nations, 2001: para 14).

These issues are further complicated by the question of whether rights can be said to exist if they are only *partially* fulfilled. The jurisprudential response to this has been to seek a compromise, with governments being allowed to work towards what is known as the 'progressive realization' of economic and social rights, while civil and political rights are in practice viewed as effectively more binding. UNDP, among others, has argued that progressive (i.e. incremental) realization is essential to be able to set development priorities. But even in this diluted form it can cause thorny legal and moral disputes, such as in the recent South African legal cases over the constitutional right to adequate housing (Roos, 2001). In effect, the language of progressive realization lets many governments off the hook (Gledhill, 2001). At the same time, some governments argue against economic and social rights on practical grounds: poor, indebted countries simply cannot afford them. This question of cost is, however, not straightforward and may be better phrased as a matter of priorities. Roger Normand, the executive director of the Centre for Economic and Social Rights in New York, for instance, argues that: 'the problem is not lack of resources but lack of political will. The same governments that find money for the latest weapons and readily grant mega-corporations enforceable economic rights cry poverty when it comes to changing the policies that consign almost half of humanity to squalor and degradation' (Normand, 2001: 16). Moreover, it can also be argued that civil and political rights can be just as costly to realize. Elections, and fair justice and policing systems, require significant resourcing, and yet political and civil rights remain at the top of the international development agenda.

In the past two decades development agencies have acquired considerable experience in rights-based work with partner governments. However, many development agencies face criticisms for failing to take their arguments to their logical conclusions, in particular to address the issue of inequality. There is a tension between the ways in which rights-based approaches have evolved away from an exclusive emphasis on civil and political rights to embrace social rights, and the neoliberal principles and policies which have been in favour over recent decades. These have sought to reduce social rights while privileging other rights such as those of property holders. Economic inequality means that, in practice, the property rights of the wealthy take precedence over the social and economic rights of the poor (Donnelly, 1999). Faced with stark indicators of increasingly unequal resource distribution and its adverse effects on human development, and evidence of the harsh consequences for the poor of economic policies (Gledhill, 2001), agencies such as DFID and UNDP have responded by advocating a more socially responsible capitalism. DFID, for example, argues strongly for a socially responsible business sector, and UNDP argues that trade negotiations should exercise a conditionality which takes human rights into account. However, while attention to business and its responsibilities is overdue, it still leaves more urgent questions of redistribution unaddressed.

Central to debates about rights and responsibilities in development is the question of the appropriate role for the state in economic regulation and wealth redistribution. While there might be formal agreement that governments are responsible for encouraging and protecting the social arrangements necessary for the full enjoyment of rights, what those arrangements might be, who benefits from these rights (citizens, the majority, non-indigenous peoples, all residents?), and how far the state should be involved, remain contentious issues.[8] NGOs working with rights among poor and marginalized groups grapple with such problems every day and, as we will see, tend to consider the state to be a major factor affecting the efficacy of rights-based programmes.

The conceptual and legal developments that have helped to promote rights-based work are significant, but their impact cannot be fully understood without analysing the local political contexts within which development agencies operate. Issues of context are crucial, as they govern the receptivity or otherwise of the premises on which these ideas are based. Ideas of rights, good governance and participation have not always been enthusiastically accepted by governments, and where they have been applied they are understood in very different ways, depending on the region and political context. For example, Morten Bøås (1998) shows that the African and Asian Development Banks are resistant to donor pressure to incorporate good governance into their lending strategies, as their member states regard conditionalities concerning political and civil rights as an infringement on their national sovereignty. In contrast, Latin America in the 1990s represented a particularly favourable context for the application of good governance agendas, with most governments giving support to the basic principles on which it rested. The following chapter illustrates this important point by outlining the main characteristics and specific features of the Latin American context over the past decade.

2 Latin America: the right(s) time and the right(s) place

Regional context

LATIN AMERICA IN THE 1990s offered a comparatively favourable opportunity context for the promotion of good governance and human rights agendas. More than half of the countries in the region were undergoing a process of 'redemocratization' or democratic consolidation following authoritarian rule (Southern Cone, Mexico, Brazil) and/or prolonged civil violence (Central America). Newly elected governments pledged themselves to introduce reforms aimed at consolidating democracy through improving institutional efficiency, representativity and accountability. This commitment to democracy and human rights was affirmed in regional meetings of institutions such as the Organization of American States, while Latin American governments signed up to the international agreements that resulted from the wave of UN summits that took place over the course of the decade.

If the incorporation of good governance issues into development policy was greeted with suspicion in some parts of the world, it was received with greater enthusiasm in Latin America. In those countries emerging from authoritarian rule there was often public and governmental support for civil and political human rights to be seen as a way of deepening the democratic process. The impunity with which many governments had acted in the past, the absence of appropriate limits on police actions, and the corruption or inefficiency of the judiciary were issues that the combined concern with democratization and human rights could address. As numerous scholars noted, post-authoritarian transitions such as occurred in Latin America were particularly favourable opportunity contexts for social movement activism around issues of democracy and justice (e.g. Jelin and Hershberg, 1996; Jaquette and Wolchik, 1998).

In Latin America, issues of rights found some natural allies within the voluntary sector. Many Latin American NGOs were disposed to support some forms of rights-based work, having themselves emerged from oppositional pro-democracy social movements. They had been able to acquire a firmer institutional basis by virtue of the increasing flows of aid they received from international donors. As public policy shifted away from reliance on the state for welfare and development towards private and voluntary agencies, NGOs grew in both number and influence in the Latin American region, following global trends. Estimates of the number of NGOs in Latin America vary, but on one assessment, in the early 1990s there were at least 11 000 working in the development sector, more than 1000 in Mexico, between 400 and 500 in Bolivia and Peru, and some 4000 in Central America (ICRC, 2001). From the mid-1980s onwards, coincident with the transition to democracy in the region, NGOs began to participate in campaigns and to develop projects that reflected a commitment to rights-based work. Among the many examples of this work can be instanced the role of civil organizations in electoral processes; the spread of legal literacy projects designed to enable low-income groups to understand and claim their rights; projects aimed at training women and indigenous people in leadership skills so that they can access political machinery; peace processes and conflict resolution; and the multiple forms of grass roots projects that sought to empower low-income groups, working with women, indigenous peoples and children in ways which drew on rights discourses to give direction to their work.

Women's NGOs became particularly active on rights issues, both working at the grass roots and lobbying governments for reform. Latin America has a long tradition of female mobilization going back to the 19th century. In the 1970s and 1980s, women's movements became active in the struggle for democracy as well as for daily survival in conditions of economic crisis. During some of the harshest moments of the dictatorships (specifically in Argentina and Chile) women mobilized to demand information about, and justice for, their 'disappeared' children. There was also a significant mobilization of low-income women across the region in response to the debt crisis and adjustment packages that hit women particularly hard. Many thousands of women became involved in activities designed to alleviate the conditions of poverty and scarcity through schemes such as the 'Glass of Milk' for children and the popular canteens, which were run by associations of women and operated at neighbourhood level. Where democracy was restored, women also became active on rights issues, demanding that governments observe the international legislation that they had signed up to following the UN Decade for Women.

A parallel development was the struggle for indigenous rights. It is worth noting that the meaning of 'indigenous' and the degree to which people identify themselves as indigenous is very variable in Latin America, where much of the population is of mixed descent. The most recent wave of indigenous organizations in the region began in the early 1970s in Ecuador, Colombia and Bolivia, inspiring similar groups throughout the region, including in Mexico (Van Cott, 1994; Stavenhagen, 2002). Many participated in the regional pro-democracy movements, gradually formulating demands and policies to guarantee indigenous rights. In the late 1980s, indigenous groups in the Americas became international actors in the fullest sense, networking globally and forging links with other global movements, notably with the environmental movement, as evidenced by the prominence of indigenous concerns at the 1992 Rio Earth Summit (Brysk, 1994). Parallel to this, and probably with more lasting political effect, indigenous peoples held several meetings across the region to prepare a coordinated response to the celebrations of the 1992 anniversary of the colonization of Latin America by Spain (Van Cott, 1994).

During the 1990s, constitutional reforms in the majority of Latin American countries gave some recognition to indigenous rights,[9] leading Donna Lee Van Cott to argue that this process constitutes 'an emerging regional model of "multicultural constitutionalism"' (Van Cott, 2000: 17). The reforms were influenced by a combination of the upsurge in indigenous political mobilization and the development of a considerable body of international jurisprudence recognizing indigenous rights as human rights. The most important instrument of the latter is the International Labour Organization's (ILO) Convention 169 (1989) which, once ratified, has the force of domestic law in signatory states. It recognizes a number of important rights, in particular the right of indigenous peoples to participate in the formulation of policies that affect them. By 2000, it had been ratified by the majority of Latin American states (Sieder, 2002: 1–4). Other notable international instruments of the 1990s were the UN Draft Declaration on Indigenous Rights (currently under review in the UN Human Rights Commission), and the Organization of American States Draft Declaration (completed in 1998 but not yet adopted) (Stavenhagen, 2002).

If post-authoritarian Latin America provided both a sympathetic environment and a receptive population for the development of rights approaches, there were three further factors that contributed to the acceptance of rights work in the region. First, the values of liberalism and democracy, while insecurely implanted and politically contested by left and right, were nonetheless the dominant cultural referents for much of the continent's modern history (see, for example, Gledhill, 1997; Molyneux, 2000a). Second, concepts of rights and entitlements were not the sole preserve of elites but have a common and popular currency going back to the colonial period. There is evidence of legal suits by poor peasants, indigenous people and even slaves in pursuit of their rights under colonial law (Chavez, 2000). Third, Latin America is a region with a comparatively vital and at times politically effective civil society. With its history of popular mobilization going back at least as far as the mid-19th century when labour movements emerged, Latin America has seen in more recent times the development of community and neighbourhood organizations, and women's and indigenous citizenship struggles. In the 1970s, demands for rights and social justice were promoted by political organizations of the Left and by Catholic radicals after the Medellin Conference (known as Vatican II), while ideas of popular participation and participatory development were also features of the period which preceded the wave of military dictatorships. The region's revolutions – in Mexico, Bolivia, Cuba and Nicaragua – also contributed to a history of popular mobilization, and advanced ideas of social justice. Nonetheless, this history of popular mobilization around rights issues was also often associated with populist political parties, with attendant authoritarian state forms and clientelistic practices. Corporatist rights and social benefits were won by some sectors of the working population at the expense of others, while advances in social rights were not always accompanied by civil and political rights (Roberts, 1995).

Since the restoration of civilian rule, political and civil rights have been extended, but social rights, notably those associated with employment and social security, have been revised and reduced in most countries. For all that has been positive in the political environment, the region remains one marked by sharp divisions between political and economic elites and marginalized majorities, with recent recovery from the recessive conditions of the 1980s having been associated with deepening income inequalities and persistent poverty. Latin America has the widest income differentials in the world, and despite the return to civilian rule, there are a number of countries with high levels of public corruption and what has been termed a 'democratic deficit' of considerable proportions (O'Donnell, 1996). Good governance, accountability and more representative political institutions remain on the reform agenda, and NGOs and civil society organizations, as noted earlier, have played an important role in pressing for change. While far from securing their objectives, they have achieved a measure of progress in helping to bring such change about.

Latin America therefore has a discontinuous and fragmented history of rights claims, which gathered momentum in the 1990s. Development practitioners could draw on an anterior experience and a broader culture of rights in refashioning their development projects in a more favourable international context. This rights culture was also constantly changing. Silvia,[10] a long standing feminist campaigner in Bolivia, with many years experience of development work in both governmental and non-governmental settings, expressed the changes as follows:

> Latin American development advocates had always highlighted rights, but the stress on *socioeconomic* rights gave way during the dictatorships to a stress on *civil and political* rights, and there was a subsequent post-authoritarian shift to *sectoral* rights [i.e. those associated with identity politics].

However, a notable development in the late 1990s was the reappearance of social and economic rights in Latin American policy debates. This was given some momentum not only by the growing concern over poverty, but also by the Vienna Conference which stressed the indivisibility of rights. Some of the regional UN agencies used this principle as a justification for introducing social rights into the policy debates over poverty alleviation. NGOs, as we shall see, also deployed the language of citizenship as a means of incorporating an integral vision of both rights (social, economic, civil, political and cultural) and participation in their advocacy work.

Brazilian theorist Evelina Dagnino argues that social movements in Latin America have used citizenship as a mobilizing concept to make demands for the extension and deepening of democracy, widening the scope of political activity from institutions to include culture. This conception of democracy 'has as a basic reference not the democratisation of the *political regime* but of society as a whole, including therefore the cultural practices embodied in social relations of exclusion and inequality' (Dagnino, 1998: 47). Her comments echo Sano's argument that governance implies democratization as a 'political culture or behavioural norm' rather than simply institutional strengthening (Sano, 2000: 736). According to Dagnino, popular movements in Brazil see part of their political struggle as confronting an 'authoritarian culture' at all levels of society. As she explains: 'urban popular movements reached this . . . understanding of the intermingling of culture and politics as soon as they realized that what they had to struggle for was not only their social rights, housing, health, education, but their very right to have rights' (Dagnino, 1998: 48). The phrase 'the right to have rights' is Hannah Arendt's, and was popularized by the Latin American women's movement during meetings held in the run-up to Beijing. When activists claimed full citizenship for women, and linked that demand to their exercise of their human rights, they were also claiming full human status for women; and in this they inherited a tradition stretching back at least as far as French feminist Olympe de Gouges and Mary Wollstonecraft in the 18th century (Wollstonecraft, 1975 [1792]; Scott, 1996; Fraser, 1999). Such a holistic view of citizenship as entailing more than formal legal rights and implying social and economic rights was increasingly articulated by NGOs against the prevailing 'exclusionary' economic strategy of the 1990s.

Despite the fact that there were a number of conditions that favoured the spread of rights-based agendas in the Latin American region, many practitioners we interviewed pointed to the negative conditions which served to undermine what could be achieved. The restoration of political liberalism in Latin America[11] was accompanied by the adoption of a new economic model premised on market-driven growth and a redefined role for the state. While this allowed a greater role for autonomous agencies in the delivery of social welfare, the rollback in public provisioning and reduction of some social rights brought increased hardship and insecurity to many. Critics questioned whether political and civil rights in the absence of adequate attention to social rights and security could provide the large numbers in poverty with a better quality of life. Economic liberalism enjoyed some notable successes in reducing inflation and promoting growth (albeit at relatively low levels) but it did not resolve problems of deprivation in Latin America and it exacerbated social inequalities. Social policy has therefore become an urgent and unresolved issue in the region (Abel and Lewis, 2002). As many NGOs argued in the UN forums of the 1990s, if rights were to have universal meaning and application, they must be accessible to all. Rights claims and legal reform could therefore not be detached from broader questions of economic management and the reform of such major sectors as health and education.

These policy shifts had a profound influence on the ways in which NGOs in the region operated. The changes in the role of the state and in the delivery of welfare altered the ways in which low-income groups formulated their demands. Whereas in the past they might have made them of the state via political representatives, they now also looked to NGOs to meet their expectations of welfare or for certain kinds of services. At the same time, state cutbacks in public expenditure, resulting in the closure or restriction of some welfare services, led to many former state sector workers entering the NGO field. Moreover, since NGO activity in Latin America developed in tandem with or grew out of social movements, there is also often considerable overlap and collaboration between NGOs and activists. With the growing institutionalization of social movements and professionalization of NGOs, activists and NGO workers have often engaged in advocacy work and some have sought governmental representation. More effective global networks have also played a part in changing the context of NGO activity: many NGO workers have close and ongoing links with social movements elsewhere in the region and in the world, and these links play an active and vital role in rights-based work (Craske and Molyneux, 2002).

Bolivia, Peru, Nicaragua and Mexico

With these general considerations concerning the Latin American context in mind, we turn now to the four countries in which the research into rights-based strategies was conducted: Bolivia, Peru, Nicaragua and Mexico. These four countries provided a variety of contexts for the development of rights-based work among low-income groups. They highlighted both the common trends in the strategies and perspectives of NGOs and the considerable breadth of approach. Our research was focused on NGOs in urban and peri-urban centres, with one case study in rural Mexico.

UN Human Development indicators show that countries from Latin America are generally towards the top of what the UN classifies as 'developing countries', although there is a marked disparity within the region. In the ranking of 88 developing countries according to the UNDP Human Poverty Index, Mexico was the 11th wealthiest, Peru was 19th, Bolivia 28th and Nicaragua 41st (Uruguay, Costa Rica, Chile and Cuba were the four highest-placed countries; no data existed for Argentina). However, poverty indicators based on averages mask the extreme disparities between rich and poor in Latin America, evidenced by some of the highest Gini coefficients in the world. On human development indicators Peru, Bolivia and Nicaragua are among the poorest countries in Latin America. Rural areas there, as elsewhere, are also considerably poorer than the urban regions. UNDP figures for GDP per capita in 2000, adjusted for purchasing power parity, estimate Peru's GDP per capita at US$4799, Bolivia's at US$2424, Nicaragua's at US$2366 and Mexico's at US$9023. For the purposes of comparison, the figure for the USA is US$34 142, Norway (ranked first in the UN Human Development Index, HDI) US$29 918, India US$2358 and Sierra Leone (ranked last in the UN HDI) US$490. Of the 173 countries ranked in the UN HDI for 2000, Mexico ranked 54th (the third Latin American country in the index), Peru 82nd, Bolivia 114th and Nicaragua 118th. Guatemala and Haiti were the only Latin American countries ranked below Nicaragua.

While average life expectancy has lengthened in Latin America, it is still low for the poorer countries in comparison to the OECD countries, which are in the upper 70s. For Peruvians it is 68, Bolivians 61.4 and

Nicaraguans 67.7, while for Mexicans it is 72.2 years. (This, however, is far higher than sub-Saharan Africa where life expectancy is 40 to 50 years.) The infant mortality rate per 1000 live births is 25 in Mexico, 40 in Peru, 62 in Bolivia and 37 in Nicaragua. Bolivia has the highest rate for this in Latin America apart from Haiti. The percentage of the total population considered to be chronically undernourished for 1997–99 was 29% in Nicaragua, 22% in Bolivia, 13% in Peru and 5% in Mexico. Here, Nicaragua was the 29th country in the list, and one of only five non-African countries in the top 30 (the other four were Haiti, Armenia, Tajikistan and Azerbaijan).

Bolivia, Peru and Nicaragua therefore rank among the poorest countries in Latin America, while Mexico, by contrast, is the second largest country in the region in terms of the size of its population and economy. All four countries have indigenous populations of varying sizes, Bolivia having the largest concentration of indigenous people at between 65 and 70% of the total population. El Alto and La Paz, where the Bolivian research was undertaken, have a high proportion of urban indigenous peoples, who have in recent years become increasingly active politically. The urban centres visited in Peru and Nicaragua have fewer indigenous organizations and a relatively smaller indigenous or indigenous-identified population overall. The Mexican case study of a rural community examined a self-identified indigenous organization.

Political environment

If the move towards rights-based strategies has focused attention on the relationship between the state and civil society, it has also underlined the importance of the prevailing political environment in each country for NGOs engaged in this work. Over recent decades, significant sectors of civil society in Latin America have evolved from being largely characterized as separate *from* (indeed opposed to) the state, to engaging *with* the state. The varying modes and outcomes of that engagement have depended on the nature of the government in question, and on the quality of the democratization process under way. This affects, to a greater or lesser extent, the feasibility of different types of rights-based strategies.

In Mexico, a country which from the early 1980s was undergoing a gradual process of democratic transition from one-party rule, NGOs formed part of an increasingly extensive mobilization in favour of democracy, political pluralism and human rights. By 1997, there were estimated to be some 3000 civil organizations in Mexico, whose autonomy from the state helped to challenge the old corporatist pacts and clientelistic practices which had characterized the rule of the Partido Revolucionario Institucional (Institutional Revolutionary Party, PRI). These civil society organizations promoted ideas of citizenship, rights and participation, and took advantage of the new opportunities granted by law to engage in debates with government agencies over reform. They therefore helped to create in Mexico a civic culture in which issues of political rights and human rights became central to the project of democratic reform, which resulted in the election of the Partido de Acción Nacional (Party of National Action, PAN) candidate Vicente Fox in 2000, ending 71 years of PRI rule.

In Nicaragua and Peru, issues of political and civil rights were coloured by the experience of revolution and civil violence. In Nicaragua, the electoral defeat in 1990 of the revolutionary party, the Frente Sandinista de Liberación Nacional (National Sandinista Liberation Front, FSLN), returned a centre-right government that reversed many of the policies of its predecessor. The post-Sandinista administration of Violeta Chamorro inherited a debt of US$10.7 billion, placing Nicaragua among the countries with the highest debt ratios in the world. Her administration and its successors pursued structural adjustment policies that impacted severely on the poor, estimated to comprise more than 50% of the population.

The extensive network of civil and political organizations established by the Sandinistas withered with their defeat, but they did not disappear. Many activists continued to work within popular organizations, while others joined or founded NGOs. Given the differences of political sympathy and divergent approaches to development work, relations between the NGO community and the three post-1990 conservative administrations were cool, sometimes tense, especially under the Alemán government as it sought to control the considerable flows of aid to the country following Hurricane Mitch in 1998. The imposition of a tax on funds received by NGOs, together with the government's choice of NGO partners, was interpreted as denying funds to certain organizations for political reasons. At the same time, post-1990 administrations' identification with conservative Catholic values put it at odds with feminist NGOs and GROs, who in turn denounced government corruption and policies. In 2002, Alemán was eventually charged with fraud and the theft of over US$4 million.

The opposition party, the FSLN, was also widely believed to have lined its pockets. At the same time, its leader, Daniel Ortega, was the subject of a scandal in which his stepdaughter, Zoilamérica Narvaez, accused him of sexual abuse from an early age. Significant sections of the women's movement called for Ortega to be brought to justice, but the pact that existed between the FSLN and the conservative administration ensured the FSLN leader's immunity. In such conditions marked by an absence of trust in politicians, there is reduced scope for cooperation between some of the most active and innovative sectors of the voluntary sector and the state. This explains why Puntos de Encuentro (discussed in Chapter 8) placed such value both on maintaining a distance from the state and on preserving its own autonomy.

In Peru, the degree of violence unleashed during the 12 years of Sendero Luminoso's campaign (1980–92) created a climate in which few civil society organizations could operate freely. Sendero's campaign of assassination of community leaders, coupled with abuses of human rights on the part of the police and army, sharply reduced citizen activism and political life. In the harsh economic conditions that prevailed in the 1980s, women's associations and NGOs in the capital, Lima, were engaged in widespread community-based feeding programmes and these continued throughout the period of civil violence. The popular canteens and the Glass of Milk programme were managed by and for low-income populations: some 10 000 women were estimated to be active in these associations.

The election of Alberto Fujimori in 1990 was followed by a crackdown on the armed rebellion and a suspension of many civil liberties, with some violations of human rights. The population tolerated or even welcomed 'strong' (i.e. authoritarian) government and Fujimori's *autogolpe*, or palace coup, of 1992 in which he suspended the constitution, dissolved congress and purged the judiciary, elicited little internal opposition. The initially popular government pursued with some success a policy of clientelistic incorporation of sectors of the population, including the women's organizations involved in the popular canteens (Blondet, 2002). As in the case of Nicaragua, the NGO sector found itself increasingly at odds with a state that adopted authoritarian and clientelistic practices in its dealings with civil society. However, Fujimori's appeal dimmed by the latter part of the 1990s, and as his administration became embroiled in large-scale corruption, the growing strength of pro-democracy forces was able to show itself in demands for his resignation. These succeeded, after initial resistance, in the closing months of 2000, as Fujimori fled to exile in Japan.

In the period since the election of Toledo in 2001, Peru, like Mexico after the election of Vicente Fox, has seen efforts to reform the state and legal system, first under the 'transitional government' and then under the new administration. NGOs are actively engaged in the reform process, presenting proposals for legal reform projects, participating in state–civil society deliberative arenas and organizing demonstrations against unpopular government initiatives. Women's groups have been especially active in the wake of a strengthening conservative Catholic influence over government policy which, as in Mexico and Nicaragua, has sought to oppose women's rights agendas in the area of reproductive rights.

Bolivia has seen significant legal reform since the early 1980s. A measure of government sympathy during the presidency of Gonzalo Sanchez de Lozada (1993–97), together with the growing strength of indigenous rights movements, led to a reform of the Constitution that explicitly recognizes the diversity of Bolivian society, its heterogeneity and its plural ethnic identity. In 1994, a process of administrative decentralization was codified into the Popular Participation Law, which, along with other reforms, granted recognition to indigenous land rights and rights of political representation. An educational reform of the same year committed the state to bilingual instruction in rural areas. Apart from its legal recognition of customary indigenous community structures, the Popular Participation Law enabled greater citizen involvement in decision making and supervision of the disbursal of local government resources. NGOs are able to consult with municipalities in the participatory design of annual operative plans, and have found a myriad of new roles in local development, as technical advisers to indigenous communities, in organization strengthening programmes and facilitating participatory planning workshops. At the same time, however, the expansion in the number of middle-class technicians in rural areas, following the relatively greater resources available locally, risks weakening local people's control over resources. Increased resources have also attracted the political parties, who have in many instances become a central part of the supposedly representative and neutral citizens' organizations.[12] The clientelistic nature of local government in particular, itself exacerbated and conditioned by the strength of political parties in the area, affects the possibilities for the development of democratic, non-clientelistic, demand making of the state on the part of civil society, in a similar way to Mexico under the PRI (Gray Molina, 2001).

The most important Bolivian NGOs appeared in the mid-1970s as voluntary organizations. Most are now funded by private foreign sources with US$100 million per annum being expended among some 800 local institutions during the 1990s (Urioste, 2001). At the time we conducted our interviews, NGO workers felt that the most important set-back for those working with such positive legal developments as the Popular Participation Law was the election of a conservative government in 1997. While the 1993–97 administration had been particularly open to NGO involvement, that of President Banzer saw many NGO advisers in government fired, and some ministries, particularly the Vice-ministry for Popular Participation, severely weakened. The lack of a non-party-political civil service in Bolivia means that changes in government at all levels result in a wholesale reorganization, structurally and in terms of personnel, and the administration and development of policies follows party political lines. This creates instability in NGOs, as people move in and out of government depending on their party political affiliation and the administration's openness to NGO lobbies. NGOs also frequently fail and new ones take their place, creating further difficulties and discontinuity. The re-election of Sanchez de Lozada to the presidency in 2002 may see a renewal of political will in favour of participatory democracy. Increased congressional representation for coca growers and indigenous groups may also provide some scope for productive state–NGO engagement.

These four cases underline the argument that the strength of governmental commitment to democratic principles conditions the nature of NGO work. This is especially so in two respects: it affects the way that issues of rights can be taken up, and it determines the degree to which NGOs can engage with the state on rights issues. Past experience of living under harsh dictatorships has affected NGO personnel's views about the desirability of cooperating with the state, and has influenced the types of political demands it is possible to make. Yet, depending on circumstances, opportunities of varying kinds are created for NGOs and community organizations to collaborate more effectively with the state. The dynamic nature of this issue was demonstrated by the strategies for cooperation with the state highlighted by our informants. These were often conditioned by the development of 'openings' within particular parts of the governmental apparatus. For example, even during the conservative government of General Banzer, some NGOs worked with sympathetic people within the Ministry of Justice in Bolivia on a human rights ombudsman scheme. In fact, the debilitation of the Popular Participation Department as a result of the change in government led to several informants seeing this as in some ways more profitable for them than working on popular participation. In 2000, citizen political participation was greatly encouraged by the National Dialogue set up by the state, under pressure from the World Bank to decide on how to distribute debt relief resources from the HIPC II initiative.[13]

The example of Bolivia highlights the importance for NGO work of the particular legislative framework and legal culture of a country. These vary between countries and through time. Decentralization initiatives have, as noted above, provided many more opportunities for NGOs to work on local demand-making processes with communities in Bolivia. With 20% of the national budget going to municipal government as of 1994, Bolivia stands in stark contrast to Peru which, until the 2002 decentralization initiative, was highly centralized, with only 6%

of the national budget going to the municipalities. As a result, Peruvian NGOs found it appropriate to work, inasmuch as they were able, with central rather than local government. States are not impermeable even if they are authoritarian; in Peru under Fujimori, the Ministry for Women and Human Development (PROMUDEH) collaborated successfully with several women's NGOs on the issue of the policing of domestic violence. In contrast, another programme, also administered by PRO-MUDEH, used soldiers as teachers in a rural literacy programme, a strategy considered by NGOs to be inappropriate and insensitive given Peru's recent history of civil violence. Under Toledo, women's net-works have sought to collaborate with sympathetic parliamentarians on aspects of the draft Constitution in which women have a special interest, such as the section on the family. Individual parliamentarians of differ-ent parties have often been important in supporting campaigns advanced through NGO advocacy, as the recent history of women's rights in Latin America demonstrates (Craske and Molyneux, 2002; Molyneux and Razavi, 2002).

The ability to exercise rights is central to the success or failure of rights-based strategies, and here structural and contextual factors play a crucial part. The variations in conditions prevailing in different Latin American countries underscore this point. A greater understanding of the factors that serve to limit or enhance rights-based work at regional, national and local levels is vital if such work is to be effective. However, differences of context should not blind us to the very real possibilities that exist for sharing good practice and discussing approaches to the common problems and benefits of rights-based work for NGOs and community organizations. In this spirit, we turn to consider some of the most innovative approaches adopted by Latin American NGOs to the rights-based agendas of recent years.

3 NGOs and rights approaches

IN THIS AND THE FOLLOWING CHAPTERS, we will consider how Latin American NGOs have responded to international development policy shifts. They have been particularly creative in designing development work that connects rights to participation and empowerment, and also in interpreting these latter concepts more broadly than is typical of most development agencies. While an important dimension of their work remains tackling social and economic exclusion, they also seek to overcome political exclusion by promoting the active participation of their users in the process of redemocratization. This involves subjective transformations through 'empowerment', as well as engaging in the debate over what democracy means and how it should be applied in practice, for example by making policy processes more accessible, transparent and accountable. In these various ways, participation is linked to governance, rights and agency, with the aim being to bring about transformations, both subjective and structural, in the conditions of subaltern groups.

Here we aim to reflect the views of NGOs, focusing on organizations for which legal themes and rights issues were often a central component of their work. However, while they all considered the provision of legal services and the pressure for legislative change central to their work, the ways in which they chose to carry this out were very varied, as Chapter 4 outlines. The majority of those who appear in this book were from women's organizations with a common commitment to working with low-income and marginalized women, paying particular attention to reproductive health, political participation, empowerment and domestic violence. The promotion of self-esteem was considered essential to each of these areas.

Welcoming rights

Given the regional conditions outlined earlier, good governance, poverty and rights were priorities that were broadly welcomed by the

NGO workers we interviewed. They shared in the prevailing consensus in favour of democratic practices and welcomed the emphasis on bottom-up, participatory approaches in development. Many endorsed the idea of integrating rights into development work, albeit with some reservations which are discussed in Chapter 4. They saw their current work as an extension and development of a long-standing commitment to the promotion of rights. This was typical of NGOs working with women. As many of these NGOs grew out of the women's movement, or drew in former activists, there has been considerable continuity in their support for rights. While they recognized the importance of recent rights-based agendas in the global arena, they did not see external pressure from donors or development agencies as the principal motor of their rights work.

Nonetheless, the issue of external influence was felt to be important in its effect on the receptivity to and perceived legitimacy of rights work. The changed international context was acknowledged to have provided support for rights work in a number of ways. UN agreements, global and regional conferences were used by NGOs to pressurize national governments. Juana, a programme director of a Peruvian NGO, stated a general view when she pointed out that working in these arenas can and does work, and that they may be the only effective resource on occasion. Human rights legislation and international protocols were seen as important, in part because of the enforcement structures that have been created, such as reporting committees or commitments to national action plans, all of which have at one time or another facilitated the mobilization of local and international pressure. However, as Sonia, a Bolivian Women's Network coordinator pointed out, they were also useful for more general standard-setting. She believed that 'summits and conferences may not have the force of law, but they have an ethical character, and imply a moral commitment from governments'.

Good governance agendas were also generally viewed positively. As expressed by Silvia, a Bolivian feminist with many years experience of activism:

> Compare countries like France or England with Bolivia. In the former two, you know what time the train leaves, what time things start, and you know that you have certain guaranteed rights to go to school, and if you're unemployed you get social security. There are rules, and even if you don't like them, at least they exist. Here we don't have any rules – Bolivia lacks political institutionality, which is a crucial theme of citizenship. You can't understand citizenship if you don't address this issue in countries like Bolivia.[14]

However, even where national legislation was seen as inadequate, or where there was scepticism about the will of governments to enforce it, many NGOs still found it possible to use rights-based strategies. Their arguments for the use of such strategies were based on both efficiency and ethical criteria. A majority of informants said simply that rights-based approaches were effective and well received among the populations with which they worked. Senior workers from all the countries involved, and with experience of direct work with communities, felt that simply discovering the existence of certain rights can be empowering. They considered that there is also some comfort in knowing that others all over the world are fighting for similar rights, thereby overcoming feelings of isolation and powerlessness. As Ana, a Bolivian project worker with nine years' experience of working with women, said:

> We find it very useful to work with national laws in particular, because the judges and lawyers are all visible, whereas international conventions are a bit nebulous for the women we work with. But we're also working on helping women to understand that there is protection for them, through universal norms. This helps them to feel more secure and less isolated. They realize that there are other countries where women are fighting for the same thing, and that we are all in the same situation.

Apart from such practical considerations, there was also a general view that rights-based strategies were simply morally appropriate, that they respected the dignity of those for whom NGOs should work, and as such were valid as an end in themselves. This reflects a distinction made in the UNDP Human Development Report of 2000, which differentiates between human rights as *means* and *ends*, stating that 'capabilities and human rights [are] ends and means of escaping poverty. . . . Human rights have intrinsic value as ends in themselves. They also have instrumental value' (UNDP, 2000: 74). UNICEF has made a similar point, as noted by Dorothy Rozga, reflecting on UNICEF's approach to rights.

> From a human rights perspective, poor people must be recognised as the key actors in their own development rather than as the beneficiaries of commodities and services provided by others. This is the essence of empowerment and for this reason, empowerment is not a 'strategy' per se, but a necessary aspect of all strategies (Rozga, 2001: 7).

In this sense then, participation links rights as means *and* ends – to rights as just means. Our informants combined this moral imperative with a view that this would provide more sustainable strategies which, in being more responsive to the priorities of poorer populations, would be more effective. Fernando, a human rights network coordinator in Bolivia, said:

> Our organization has a mission, which is the construction of a new paradigm, that of human rights and democracy. We think that working for the defence and explanation of human rights takes our society on the road to a participatory democracy, where there is real participation of the population, in articulating not only social but also political demands about how they want development to be implemented.

Julia, a director of a children's rights network in Peru, saw rights-based approaches as important because they could stimulate a change in mentalities: 'seeing a person not only as a person with needs, but as a person with rights, allows people to see themselves as citizens'. She also believed that a rights focus in development had two main practical benefits: first, permitting through the careful use of indicators the establishment of goals for better development; and second, promoting respect for different cultures, an increasingly central issue in those parts of Latin America with indigenous and/or black populations.

Rights and needs

Such endorsements of rights-based approaches do not, however, imply a neglect of needs issues as is sometimes claimed. Many NGO practitioners felt it important to develop a poverty-focused approach to rights. If they criticized projects that worked to satisfy narrow conceptions of needs, they were also reluctant to embrace a narrow vision of formal rights that did not address material needs. For many, the issue was not how to shift from needs to rights, but how to combine them. This was important, since the conceptual distinctions between needs and rights were not always clearly drawn. Needs were often expressed in terms of rights, as in the need for (or right to) information, capacity building, health and education.[15]

However, many organizations have experienced a discernible move away from a focus on practical daily needs towards strategic aims, which were usually defined in terms of rights. Ana said: 'Women have always known about their daily needs, but they've not been given information about their rights or anything else', and this knowledge gap is something that most of the organizations in this study aimed to redress in one way or another. The idea that needs and rights were linked was expressed by another programme director for the same organization, who believed that in general there had occurred a move from needs to rights discourses, but insisted that such a move should not be at the expense of ignoring the needs and demands of the population. In effect, as she said, 'these needs are really nothing more than rights that are not being exercised'. While the close link between needs and rights was acknowledged, the difference between the two concepts is a significant one. Rights imply agency, an active subject who enjoys a certain set of entitlements or guarantees before the law (see Cornwall and Gaventa, 2000). In this sense rights are potentially empowering and their denial or lack of substantive meaning can form the basis for action. As Sonia Corrêa points out:

> 'Rights' will always imply the capacity to make autonomous decisions, to assume responsibilities and to fulfil needs, both in the individual and the collective sense. The construction of rights implies the re-balancing of power relations and a horizon of justice. The notion of rights refers to the relationship of the subject with her/himself, and the relationship between individuals and collectivities (societies, states, markets) (Corrêa, 1997: 111).

Some informants made a distinction between a rights focus and a health focus, which they saw as responding to needs. Amy, a worker with an NGO specializing in legal literacy, pointed out that:

> Many sexual or reproductive health projects, or projects about domestic violence, run the risk of only having a health perspective, and not one of human rights. So they centre on the quality of services but not on the exercising of rights as claims for justice, and even less on demands that the state fulfil its responsibility. This means that responsibility is privatized.

Others argued that a good quality of attention in health services should be seen as a right. Rights discourses can expose contradictions in dominant ethical and legal norms. In the above remarks Amy was arguing that human rights could be used to make claims against the (neoliberal) reduction of state welfare expenditure, in her appeal for more state responsibility in the health sector. While theorists dispute the potential for using rights in a counter-hegemonic way (Scott, 1999; Stammers, 1999; Evans, 2000), the issue of health provides one example where advocates attempt to confront prevailing policies with alternative demands. All governments are selective in the kinds of rights they choose to implement, but where rights are recognized by the international community, there are opportunities for criticism and contestation. As Subrahmanian has written: 'Recasting issues conventionally understood to constitute the realm of human need (such as basic entitlements of food and shelter) in terms of human rights is a strategic move to prevent the conflation of basic services with welfare programmes targeting beneficiaries through handouts and not economic redistribution' (Subrahmanian, 2002: 21).

In sum, rights approaches have been taken to imply an emphasis on empowerment and participation, on the right of the poor to define their own needs, and to take an active part in their own development. Rights were also seen as providing a structure within which this kind of claim making becomes possible, at least in theory. The individual subject of rights was viewed as a recognized and integral part of an internationally adopted system of law. This influences and structures the strategies available to NGOs within the broad remit of rights-based work.

4 Implementing rights: participation, empowerment and governance

IN THIS CHAPTER we illustrate the centrality of two characteristics of rights discourses in the implementation of rights-based development approaches in Latin America: first, the foregrounding of the idea of empowerment; and second, the focus on *strategic effect*, namely the social impact on the wider community. The most innovative NGOs translate human rights philosophies into practical action in the field in a number of ways and on various levels. Among the most significant that we found were:

- encouraging people to assume their rights on a personal, subjective level
- strengthening popular organizations so that people can make their own demands
- working directly with agents of the state to create and/or strengthen legal mechanisms
- applying political pressure through lobbying and campaigning.

The first two points are considered as examples of empowerment work on different levels, while the second two are discussed as strategic attempts to improve the instrumental efficiency and democratic accountability of the state, and to promote the rule of law and good governance.

Linking participation, empowerment and rights

The idea of empowerment has a wide application in Latin American NGO work. The 'empowerment approach' was widely adopted in the 1980s and has become a central conceptual tool for NGOs working with low-income groups and with women (Goetz, 1991). Stromquist proposes that empowerment consists of four dimensions: the cognitive (critical understanding of one's reality), the psychological (feeling of self-esteem), the political (awareness of power inequalities and the ability to organize and mobilize) and the economic (capacity to generate independent income) (Stromquist, 2002: 23). Townsend et al. (1999), following the work of Rowlands (1998), discuss power in four modalities: power over, power from within, power to and 'power with'. Their case studies of projects in Mexico provide accounts of women's journeys from a world described in terms of obstacles to one where they have become agents of their own lives, in accounts that accord with our findings. We outline here how the NGOs in our study attempted to develop 'power from within' for their target groups, which they saw as dependent on 'power with', that is the power of cooperation and collective action.

Feeling right(s)

Most organizations had a fairly loose definition of rights, appealing to international legal instruments and national legislation when useful and strategically appropriate, but usually starting from a personal, intuitive idea of the inherent rights of human beings. In general terms, they shared the view expressed by Natalia, a Bolivian programme director, that rights are not just legal rights, but part of 'daily life, personal emotional environment, work environment and human relations'. She thought that the women's movement needed to ' "desanctify" rights, and make them less formal'. Others felt that rights could be too abstract or theoretical, although a few considered their relevance to daily life as a strength of rights strategies. One trainer of human rights 'promoters' (teachers/facilitators) in Nicaragua maintained that: 'It is even easier to start talking to people about rights than about gender. This is because they see the law as a useful instrument, which has to do directly with their lives.' This is one of the most distinctive contributions that experienced development practitioners can bring to current donor understandings of rights strategies, which generally fail to consider the personal and day-to-day implications of rights for those who are involved in development projects.

NGOs saw an important part of their work as changing attitudes through the use of rights discourses, and central to this was the focus on the individual subject noted earlier. Many of our informants highlighted the importance of people seeing themselves as having rights, arguing, for example, that 'if you do not see yourself as a person who

Box 1   Rights and daily life: El Alto, Bolivia

A key strategy in rights work in Latin America has been making rights relevant to people's daily lives. A good example of an NGO using such a strategy is the work of the 'Psycho-legal' programme unit of the Centro de Promoción de la Mujer Gregoria Apaza, which works in District 6 of the City of El Alto, Bolivia. Having decided that its fundamental strategy would be to make rights relevant on a personal level, this unit gave both legal and psychological attention to individuals and groups. It focused on violence against women, seeing legal cases through the judicial system, and counselling female victims of violence.

In addition, it ran a course to train legal educators, aiming to use the knowledge gained in the process to help other women of El Alto. The content of this course was made directly relevant to the women's daily lives. For example, the session one author attended explained how to register children. Increasing the numbers of children who are legally registered at their birth has been an important part of the campaign for children's rights, influenced by the UN Convention on the Rights of the Child, since formal registration is necessary for the provision of an identity card and the various legal entitlements it allows. The workshop started with an exploration of the ideas of what rights children have at different ages, drawing from participants' own views, but with the course facilitator adding issues/rights she felt had been left out. The course followed a participatory methodology, involving the author, soliciting her opinion on different issues and including her in the role-plays, etc. Referring specifically to the national legislative code for children, the facilitator dealt with its contents and the costs, processes and reasons for registering children, particularly for single mothers. The course participants were given explanatory leaflets to take home with them.

is a subject with rights, nothing will change'. The way to work was not seen purely in terms of increased or better information on rights, but in terms of strategies to achieve a personal capacity to exercise rights.

NGOs working with women gave particular emphasis to the importance of working to promote self-esteem as one of the goals of empowerment. In publicity materials, they declared their objectives to be greater autonomy and self-confidence for women and young people. Some NGOs did this through the provision of direct legal services to individual users. GIN, CIDEM and Gregoria Apaza – organizations for women and children – all provided psychological consultations, and counselling; and Manuela Ramos ran a health consultancy.[16] For all these organizations, services were generally focused around the issue of violence against women and children. Most of the NGOs discussed here, however, did not provide direct services of this type, but addressed the issues of consciousness raising and self-esteem in educational workshops. Some specifically worked in training networks of popular educators, in human rights and/or health issues. TAREA (an education-based NGO in Peru) produced educational materials for the state educational system at primary, secondary and teacher training levels (see Box 11). Box 1 illustrates an example of the link between self-esteem and the exercise of rights.

Demanding rights

The realization of individual and personal capabilities was predominantly viewed as possible through group action – 'power with' in Rowlands' terms (1998). Work on the personal level, such as that described above, was seen as inherently linked to the strengthening of popular organizations. NGOs in Latin America have to consider carefully their role in civil society, and their relationships with social movements. This can be a difficult issue for feminist NGOs, which are a vital part of the women's movement, but which claim that role based on an oft-criticized ability to represent others – 'the grass-roots' (Mohanty, 1991a). Moser et al. (2001: 45) highlight some characteristics of 'effective pro-poor advocacy institutions', arguing that 'the evidence suggests that without external assistance the poorest and most marginalized will generally lack the capacity to negotiate effectively for their rights'. They suggest that such 'external assistance' should 'listen to [the poor's] views and adapt to their priorities and realities'. In Latin America, high levels of community mobilization have meant that one of the ways NGOs provide such 'external assistance' is through technical support for community organizations, one example of which is described in Box 2.

Recent years have seen the emergence of NGOs that view their role as supporting community/grass-roots organizations (GROs). The two case studies in Chapter 8 give greater detail about such developments. Box 3 provides an example of a Peruvian NGO that defines itself in terms of the educational support it provides for women's community organizations.

While some organizations considered their role as purely one of supporting community organizations, it was more common for NGOs to use such work as part of an overall strategy. This has been the path followed by other large women's NGOs in Lima, such as Flora Tristan

Box 2   Organizational strengthening

TAHIPAMU, a small NGO based in La Paz, Bolivia, developed a strong relationship with the Federation of Women Domestic Workers, providing capacity building, advice, help with campaign materials and lobbying support. During the five years that TAHIPAMU worked with the Federation, the latter changed a great deal, although the worker in charge did not attribute these changes solely to TAHIPAMU's influence. She felt that much was due to the women's own experiences, and some to their relationships with NGOs other than TAHIPAMU. Nonetheless, in her opinion, the Federation's capacity for negotiation became more sophisticated; they were less intransigent, and were able to create and work with allies in parliament. They also developed a more integral approach to their work.

Box 3   Capacity building

Since 1992, FOVIDA has been running a school for women leaders of community organizations, predominantly those focused on basic food provision, such as communal kitchens. Their educational objectives illustrate the combination of self-esteem work with practical aims:

'**In the personal dimension**, that women reinforce their own processes of personal autonomy, and the positive valuing of their own image, giving particular attention to their subjectivity, and making them recognise and process feelings that affect their health and sexuality. This will permit them to identify their own spaces and strategies for a better position in the gender relations that they establish.

'**In the functional dimension**, the development of the capacity to carry out different management jobs; analysing the objective world, which permits them to formulate visions for the future in terms of organisational and technical progress, and of citizenship participation' (Cáceres Valdivia et al., 1998: 18–19).

Their capacity-building materials are visually attractive and participatory, using discussion exercises based on personal experiences as a woman and as a leader of an organization. They cover such themes as health, strategic planning, business, nutrition and gender.

As a result of reflecting on their work, those in charge at FOVIDA decided to become more involved in local development; but they remained focused on developing and encouraging women's leadership. Central to this was the facilitation of women's analysis of their social situation and their consequent politicization.

and Manuela Ramos. The decision to undertake this kind of work in part responded to the philosophical and political approaches of activists, and in part was a result of donor pressure for more strategic approaches. DFID, for example, has stated that it will channel its resources for gender equality more towards 'supporting fundamental changes in policy, laws, and attitudes', while maintaining (only) 'strategic links with work at the grassroots' (DFID, 2000a: i). Central, however, was the changing local political context. NGOs in Bolivia formulated such strategies in response to changes in local development planning, instituted in the mid-1990s, as Box 4 shows.

NGO projects aimed at supporting community organizations deserve more research, in order to examine the problems and benefits that might result, and to identify best practice. There are certainly some concerns about representativity, particularly if middle-class intellectual and technical NGOs are creating yet more layers between donors and recipients of aid. On the other hand, such NGO mediation may mean that more community organizations are able to gain access to funds and technical support from external sources.

Our informants tended to consider it a political imperative to strengthen community organizations, one which resulted from a commitment to rights-based approaches. The objective of strengthening the possibilities for people to make their own demands through their own organizations connects participation and empowerment to rights in practical ways, aiming to *implement* people's fundamental rights to speak and to self-determination.

Governance and the rule of law

Working with the state

As noted earlier, NGOs use human rights and citizenship rights as organizing concepts around which to engage with the state. The type of work that our informants most readily conceptualized as human rights work developed from an imperative to institutionalize human rights in the ways envisaged by human rights legislators at international level: a UN Declaration becomes an International Covenant, which is followed by national ratification, and the design and implementation of appropriate legislation at national levels (see Chapter 5). This section discusses the final step in that process.

UN and donor agencies have identified an important role for themselves in encouraging effective national legislation to protect human

---

Box 4   Gaining voice and presence: demand making at local government level

Several organizations surveyed in Bolivia worked on local development, particularly in relation to the Popular Participation Law (*Ley de
Participación Popular*, LPP). One of these was the local development
unit of the Centro de Promoción de la Mujer Gregoria Apaza. They
worked with neighbourhood, women's and school organizations in
El Alto to develop proposals for incorporation into the participatory
planning processes mandated under the LPP, that feed into the municipality's Annual Operational Plan (*Plan Operativo Anual*, POA). Their
aims were to ensure that women and young people had a voice in these
local development processes.

As such, they responded to the kinds of demands expressed by
Ana, the director of this programme:

> [the women say] 'I have the right to speak. I don't speak
> because I don't know how, but I know that I have the right to
> do so.' 'So, this is a demand' we say, 'that we have to meet so
> that you can speak, in order to intervene and to be someone.'

Gregoria Apaza completed a participatory research diagnosis of
District 6 in the city of El Alto in 1997 (Centro de Promoción de la
Mujer Gregoria Apaza, 1997), and used information gained from this
to feed into the process of developing strategic proposals for the
POAs. They also saw themselves as facilitators, holding workshops
to encourage women and young people to voice their own demands
and needs. In addition, they ran courses seeking to encourage
women's leadership and knowledge of the law, particularly the LPP.

---

rights. For example, the Human Rights Strengthening Program
(HURIST), which is a link programme between the UNHCHR and
UNDP, initially focused its rights-based development work on helping
governments to produce national human rights action plans, although it
has since recognized the need to extend its scope (van Weerelt, 2001).
However, many of our informants pointed out the need for the effective *implementation* of existing legislation, so that people are able to
exercise their rights, and rights can therefore move off the paper to
become meaningful. In recent years, there have been more opportunities for NGOs in Latin America to collaborate with governments in this
process, albeit with a number of problems for those organizations that
see themselves as more than just implementers of government policy.
Some of these issues are discussed in Chapter 6.

The majority of the NGOs we investigated worked with some state authorities, ranging from the police and judicial systems, to municipal government, health personnel, legislators, teachers and national civil servants. For the NGOs themselves, the chief means of engaging with the state were through raising cases with the relevant legal authorities, conducting campaigns among civil servants, collaborating on a local level for local development purposes and capacity-building workshops for state employees. Work in collaboration with government authorities was a recent development for many NGOs and was largely entered into tentatively. The most important thematic entry points for NGO–state collaboration were violence against women, health (particularly the quality of services) and local development. Some organizations also worked within the educational system, particularly capacity building among teachers. Flora Tristan has taken the unusual step of helping to set up a Masters degree in gender studies at San Marcos University in Lima. A good proportion of the young men and women who take the degree also become active on some of Flora's campaigns. SERPAJ (Servicio Paz y Justicia, Peace and Justice Service) in Nicaragua worked in the prison system on the theme of non-violent conflict resolution. These kinds of activities are not peculiar to Latin America, for example Naripokkho, a Bangladeshi women's NGO, sits on several government–NGO committees on gender and reproductive health (Huq, 2000). Box 5 describes the activities of one well established women's NGO in Peru.

NGO practitioners are acutely aware of the risks and problems associated with working with government agencies – risks which varied from country to country. However, many we spoke to felt that this collaboration was a necessary step. As Shireen Huq points out, engagement with the state, wherever this may be, is neither automatic nor easy, and relies on activists being prepared to contribute ideas and work hard in demanding space for engagement.

> Although it is recognized that the state is not monolithic, the democratic space to engage with it is neither guaranteed nor always available. The identification of allies and potential allies within government can facilitate constructive engagement with the state, but it is ultimately the preparedness of activists to contribute ideas and information and their willingness to work hard and long hours that accord the space to do so (Huq, 2000: 78).

Yet in some cases, effective openings do exist, and where this was not the case, our informants thought that governments were still susceptible to international pressure. Furthermore, they considered that certain actions were ultimately the state's responsibility, and that the state

Box 5   Good practice in policing: gender training

Flora Tristan (Flora) was the first feminist NGO established in Peru. Since 1989, it has been collaborating with the national police on the theme of violence against women. It had a legal consulting service for female victims of violence in the Lima police station for women, but also ran capacity-building and sensitizing courses for police officers in collaboration with PROMUDEH, the Ministry for Women and Human Development under Fujimori. Attendance at one of its courses became part of the promotion mechanisms within the police force.

The three-day course attended by one of the authors was significantly larger than Flora Tristan had expected, with 130 participants. It was therefore less participatory than it could have been, and there was not enough time to fully complete all the modules. It was structured in terms of lectures and group work. The group work addressed the quality of attention in police stations and the legal procedures for police officers dealing with a charge of intra-family violence. These provoked much discussion, and all the police officers that the author talked to at the time found it highly informative.

The majority of those attending were men, and many were of a high rank. Many had been obliged to attend as the representative of their police station. A large minority came from rural areas of Peru. The geographical coverage was impressive, and the officers took away detailed materials, including copies of the relevant laws, models for charge sheets and a copy of the Convention of Belem do Pará, the Latin American elaboration of the UN Declaration on Violence Against Women.

Ten percent of those present had attended a previous two-month course on intra-family violence, and were therefore beginning to become specialized in this area. However, the most important problem for Flora, apart from the size of the police force in Peru (90 000), was the fact that the police rotate jobs frequently, making it difficult to gain expertise in any one area, and implying the need to start from scratch each time. Nonetheless, those police officers who attended the course had been made aware of the issue of intra-family violence and relevant legislation, and could in the future apply this awareness to all areas of their policing practice.

could achieve greater national coverage in comparison with private institutions. However, conscious and careful working with the state could lead to greater sustainability and effectiveness in NGO work. While they were well aware of the risks and realities of cooptation, an issue discussed in Chapter 6, Latin American NGOs have a strong base from which to work with the state if they retain their autonomous identity, collaborating and criticizing as appropriate. This possibility has resulted from the greater legitimacy enjoyed by the now mature women's movement, as well as other social movements, coupled with the support NGOs can draw on from international networks, donors, the UN and the international community.

Lobbying and campaigning for rights

In these various ways, NGOs were promoting the rule of law and political 'institutionality', acting within the framework of good governance discussed in Chapter 1. In addition, though, they were aiming to institutionalize 'new' human rights through legislation. As Fernando explained, 'we have to pressurize [the government] so that those rights that aren't yet legislation become part of national law in the future'. NGOs fought for such rights, utilizing those rights already recognized in their campaigns. In this way, they attempted to change the political cultures of the societies in which they operated. Public awareness campaigns (for example about violence against women and children's rights) were linked to lobbying parliamentarians for specific legislation. Yet they viewed their target 'political culture' not simply as the preserve of Congress members or civil servants, but also as involving the media and civil society more generally. Civil society has, in Alvarez et al.'s (1998) formulation, become 'both terrain and target' for social movement activism.

All the NGOs we investigated worked to raise public awareness in some way, combining in their institutional aims general attitude change and legislative or policy change. Strategies included publishing and distributing materials, such as posters, leaflets or magazines, holding public forums, such as debates, teach-ins and other events, developing Internet resources, broadcasting on local radio programmes and publishing articles in newspapers, as well as direct lobbying of parliamentarians. One NGO (Puntos de Encuentro in Nicaragua) prepared a TV soap opera and had its own channel on cable TV. Others have set up radio programmes, sometimes operating only at local district level. Boxes 6 and 7 highlight two specific examples.

A number of NGOs use international human rights legislation to frame their public awareness and lobbying campaigns. Their campaigns have relied on an articulation between national and international levels of political and legislative activity. NGO lobbying at these diverse levels is a crucial part of the process that results in UN declarations

---

Box 6   Citizenship: international and national

CIDEM, based in La Paz, Bolivia, held a public forum in the run-up to the presidential elections of 1997 entitled 'Towards the Full Citizenship of Women'. It invited all the candidates to give a 15-minute presentation on their party's proposals for the implementation of the Beijing Platform for Action. All the candidates accepted the invitation, except, ironically, Hugo Banzer, who was ultimately successful. The organizers nonetheless considered it a success, as all of those invited had had to read and consider the Platform for Action. In addition, it achieved widespread publicity for feminist concerns.

Box 7   Empowerment and the market

Since 1989, DEMUS of Lima, Peru, has developed a project about sexist advertising. Initially taking the form of denouncing advertisements that degrade women, it expanded to include discrimination more generally, for example discrimination on the basis of race or class. Thus, DEMUS made new alliances with indigenous and Black organizations. It took discrimination cases, such as that of a nightclub which refused entry to indigenous people, to INDECOPI, the office funded by the World Bank, to enforce the free market and consumer rights. This strategy helped to widen the scope of action for the Peruvian feminist movement. New targets for political pressure have emerged and new allies have been found, such as consumer organizations. In this way, DEMUS felt it had used the principle of a free market to protect the rights of women, indigenous peoples and Black people. DEMUS materials regarding sexist advertising used CEDAW, the Convention of Belem do Pará and national legislation to back up its case. It provided details on how to complain about offensive adverts to INDECOPI, and offered advice on presenting specific complaints.

---

or programmes for action that arise from international conferences. Individual countries ratify declarations or sign plans of action. After a certain number have ratified declarations, they can become international law, in the form of covenants. Ratification signals a determination on the part of national government to enshrine the international covenant in national law, but this does not always happen in practice (Fraser, 1999). In many instances, there are regional covenants, e.g. on indigenous rights, that lie between UN and national levels. At all these different

Box 8　NGOs and the UN

In 1996, Flora Tristan prepared its own report on the situation of women in Peru and presented it to the UN Committee on Civil and Political Rights. Their report 'shadowed' the official document submitted by the Peruvian government. It was a bold move, as at that time Flora Tristan did not have official consultative status to the UN, and was unfamiliar with the appropriate formats for such reports or how to present them. Overcoming its apprehension about dealing with such an important body as the UN, it found the Committee helpful, and much of its information formed part of the official UN recommendations to the government. As a result, some Peruvian legislation was altered, and Flora Tristan became the only national NGO in Peru with consultative status to the UN. At the time of research, it was preparing a shadow report for the UN committee reporting on CEDAW.

Such a strategy was considered appropriate to Peru for a number of reasons. Many Peruvian NGO workers maintained that the national government was particularly concerned about its international image. Another NGO director added that, on occasion, international pressure was the only way to influence the government: as with most countries, Peru did not want to be seen as either too radical or as lagging behind. Furthermore, Flora Tristan's report to the UN provided it with an opportunity for large-scale publicity within Peru, fulfilling awareness-raising imperatives there. In addition, the Peruvian government of the time was less than thorough in its reporting to the UN on CEDAW, often using old data, for example. Flora Tristan felt that its shadow report would not only provide the UN with a better picture, but might also push the government into taking the reporting process more seriously. Some activists argue that such activities are set to become more frequent, as the Optional Protocol to the 'Women's Convention' approaches full legal status (Fraser, 1999; Tang, 2000).

stages of the process, NGOs are involved in lobbying activities. Then, once national legislation is in draft or in place, they can use the law to influence public opinion. DEMUS in Peru decided on a strategy of taking up precedent-setting legal cases, as a means both of pushing the law further and of gaining publicity for its campaigns. Other organizations chose to influence public opinion through the media. Puntos in Nicaragua, for instance, used its own radio shows and popular magazine to debate legal issues. Still more consciousness-raising activities coalesced around ensuring that the law was workable, such as those explained in previous sections. These processes are not exclusive to Latin America, as women's NGOs all over the world use similar tactics (Fraser, 1999; Huq, 2000; Petchesky, 2000). NGOs have also appealed directly to international legal mechanisms for the enforcement of human rights in support of their aims. Box 8 details one example of this.

However, public pressure and lobbying are not without their challenges: informants battled against ingrained attitudes among the public and politicians and a generalized ignorance of rights (or scepticism) within the population. For some, participation in international initiatives was overly costly and time-consuming. One of the Nicaraguan NGO coordinators for the Fourth World Conference on Women spoke of the amount of work involved in convening meetings on a national scale and producing various materials, which included translations of what she felt was unnecessarily obscure UN language. Overall she felt that it represented 'high costs and dubious benefits for the organization'.

5 Campaigning for rights: violence against women and women's citizenship

IN THIS CHAPTER we discuss two themes that have been central to rights work in Latin America – the Violence against Women (VAW) campaign, and citizenship, both of which have been promoted by the women's movement across the region. We begin by examining the campaign for attitude change and appropriate legislation on violence against women as an example of one of the most successful rights-based campaigns in recent years. Using a specific campaign in this way enables us to illustrate the practical ways in which development NGOs have implemented rights-based approaches, combining advocacy and practical work at various political levels to push for both legal reform and the effective exercise of women's rights in a particular area.

In the second part of this chapter, we turn to the issue of women's citizenship, which was particularly important for the Latin American regional preparations for the Beijing Fourth World Conference on Women. After 1995, the Latin American women's movement began annual celebrations of Women's Citizenship Day, on 8 September. These served to highlight women's demands and to pressurize governments to fulfil the objectives of the national plans of action they drafted when they signed up to international conventions.

While the VAW campaign is by now well established, and one on which the UN has taken a strong lead at this stage of its maturity, advocacy in favour of full citizenship for women (conceived in post-Beijing terms) is at an earlier, and perhaps more vulnerable, stage. Differing ideas about citizenship in terms of practical action for development illustrate the ways in which the 'empowerment approach' of the 1970s, referred to earlier, has evolved in combination with strategic and good governance agendas. The two campaigns are linked by the connections being made between the ability to exercise rights in the private and public spheres. In terms of citizenship theory, the VAW campaign

Figure 1   Four sites of action: the interrelationship between different
types of NGO work and international, regional and national legislation,
using the example of Violence Against Women

From global to national
Across all levels, NGOs work to change public opinion and cultural attitudes
to violence against women, through lobbying, publicity, educational
workshops, academic research, etc.

I GLOBAL

Global women's movement lobby
Using recommendations of UN
conferences on women, experiences
of women's organizations globally,
academic research, etc.

**UN Declaration on Violence
Against Women (1993)**

Juridical process

II REGIONAL

**International regional networks
and national women's
organizations lobby for regional
legal instrument**
Using same tools, plus UN declaration

**Convention of Belem
Do Pará (1994)**

Juridical process

III NATIONAL

**National women's movements
lobby for ratification**
Using same tools plus Belem do Pará

**Ratification at
national level**

Juridical process

**National organizations lobby
parliamentarians, and are also
sometimes involved in designing
legislation**
Using all above plus fact of
ratification

National legislation
e.g. Ley de Violencia
Intrafamiliar, Bolivia

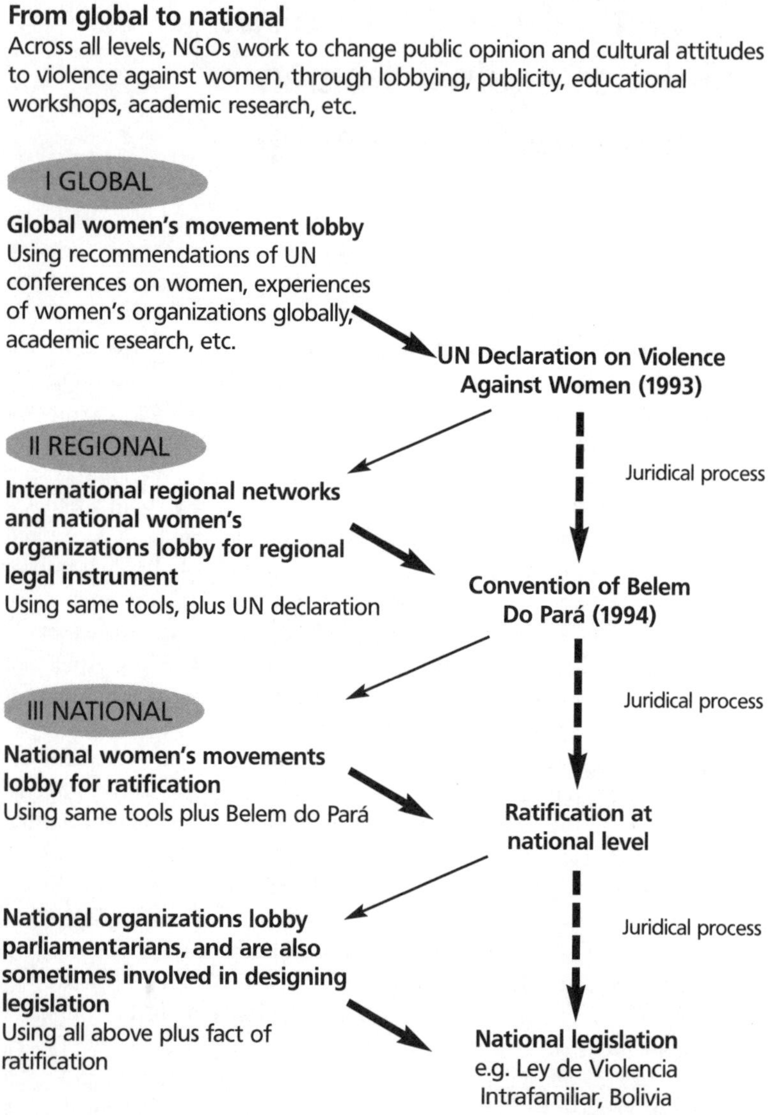

From national to individual
Work on changing public opinion and cultural attitudes to VAW continues

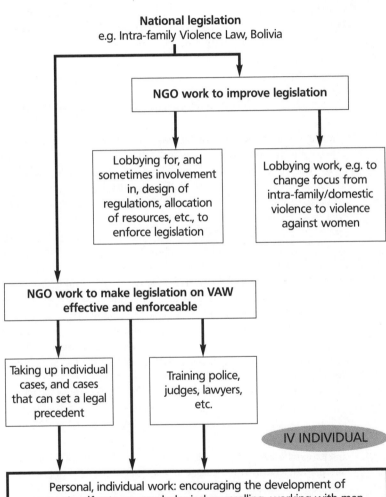

III NATIONAL

National legislation
e.g. Intra-family Violence Law, Bolivia

NGO work to improve legislation

Lobbying for, and sometimes involvement in, design of regulations, allocation of resources, etc., to enforce legislation

Lobbying work, e.g. to change focus from intra-family/domestic violence to violence against women

NGO work to make legislation on VAW effective and enforceable

Taking up individual cases, and cases that can set a legal precedent

Training police, judges, lawyers, etc.

IV INDIVIDUAL

Personal, individual work: encouraging the development of women's self-esteem, psychological counselling, working with men, legal advice, helping with the development of personal strategies to overcome individual situation of violence, plus educational workshops for women and men confronted the public/private separation central to classical liberalism and insisted that the family did not remain outside the sphere of justice. As expressed by Guatemalan sociologist Ana Cecilia Escobar, 'we exercise citizenship to the extent that we are able to interact as subjects among ourselves, with the State, and with civil society. This process must include the politicisation of the private sphere, which has to do with individual rights and access to the world that is considered public' (Isis International Documentation and Information Center, 1998). What both campaigns have in common is the way they put the individual subject of rights at the centre of a complex web of personal, local and global relationships.

'A life free of violence. It's our right', the VAW campaign

The VAW campaign effectively combined work for legal reform with grass-roots involvement. It acquired a global reach through trans-national networking active throughout Latin America. It was also able to achieve a broad consensus, allowing strategic alliances between otherwise opposed groups such as feminist organizations and the churches. By the end of the 1990s, all the Latin American countries had signed up to CEDAW, the UN Convention on the Elimination of All Forms of Discrimination Against Women. The Vienna conference acknowledged women's right to protection against domestic violence, the culmination of years of struggle by women's movements across the world for the dignity and recognition of women. This was the issue that inspired one of the most popular and effective campaigns ever to have been promoted by Latin American women's movements. NGOs that worked with rights-based agendas joined with organizations pressuring the state for legal reform and were able to collaborate productively on these issues, securing support for women's refuges and changes in the law. As a result of the work of local and transregional networks the majority of countries set about reforming antiquated national legislation and introduced a range of policies to deal with domestic violence.

The campaign on VAW illustrates a central contention of this book, which is that Latin American NGOs are adept at conceptualizing their mission from the bottom up. The most successful NGOs we spoke with placed their target populations at the heart of a system of rights, with implications and ramifications from the personal level through to the global. Figure 1 represents schematically the types of work and relationships that developed throughout this system with regard to VAW. It is a simplification of the complex processes and relationships that developed during recent years, and can be seen as summarizing the work of the different organizations that took part in this study. It also illustrates the translation of the idea of citizenship into practical agendas for action.

Figure 1 illustrates the interaction between international (global and regional) legislation, and national legislation and action by NGOs on the ground. We can map the connections between different bodies of legislation around violence against women, from the UN Declaration (1993) to the regional Convention of Belem do Pará (1994), through to national laws in each of the countries studied. NGOs lobbied at the international level for appropriate UN declarations and regional conventions, then at national level for ratification and legislation. They then used the national legislation as an advocacy tool to work towards its effective enforcement. This framework is combined with work at community level to develop women's self-esteem and personal strategies for overcoming intra-family violence.

From the global to the local

The United Nations interagency initiative 'Campaign for Women's Human Rights', with the slogan '*una vida sin violencia es un derecho nuestro*' ('A life free of violence. It's our right'), was promoted as part of the commemoration of the 50th anniversary of the Universal Declaration of Human Rights in campaigns run in Latin America, the Caribbean, Africa and Asia-Pacific between December 1997 and March 1999. Headed by UNIFEM, the UN agencies involved were UNDP, UNFPA, UNICEF, UNHCR, UNHCHR, UNAIDS and ECLAC.[17] In Spanish-speaking Latin America, the above slogan could be found on posters prominently displayed in most of the NGOs we visited as part of the research for this book. The campaign was implemented in diverse ways in the 19 Latin American countries involved. In general, activities sponsored by the UN included media campaigns of press releases, articles, interviews and stories, training programmes for government officials, the police and the army, public awareness campaigns and national reports. Of course, the campaign was not restricted to those activities directly sponsored by the UN, and it took on a life of its own, which continued past the official end of the UN campaign in March 1999.

In 2001, UNIFEM launched a similar regional advocacy campaign in eight countries of the Commonwealth of Independent States (CIS) and Lithuania. Since 1996, UNIFEM has run the Trust Fund in Support of Actions to Eliminate Violence Against Women, using it to support innovative projects worldwide, with grants from $25 000 to $120 000 in 2002, and a total expenditure of $1 million, spread over 18 programmes (UNIFEM, 2002).

It is not possible to provide a linear narrative of the 1998–99 VAW campaign in Latin America. As with other rights issues, activists operated on various levels: personal, local, national, subregional, regional and global, as illustrated in Figure 1. However, there are several notable aspects of the VAW campaign which inform our analysis of the possibilities for coherent rights-based work in development, as presented in Chapter 4. These are:

- the articulation between media campaigning, lobbying and legal reform
- the centrality of research projects to successful activism
- the role of training of government personnel for the effective implementation of legal reforms
- the importance of practical, personal work with target populations.

The campaign website for the Andean region of UNIFEM[18] highlights the production of awareness-raising materials for the communications media, including a website, a magazine (*María María*), reporting and photographic competitions, advertising 'spots', workshops, meetings, seminars, exhibitions and public posters. Notable initiatives include the production of postage stamps in Ecuador depicting the campaign slogan and graphic, and the inclusion of the slogan on telephone bills in El Salvador. Linking the media and public awareness-raising objectives with attempts to directly influence state institutions, they also ran competitions to recognize municipalities that promote women's participation in 1998, 1999–2000 and 2001. Their strategy of bringing together representatives from candidate municipalities was important for the sharing of experience and good practice at supra-national level. In the Andean region, UNIFEM attributes the 1998 adoption of the Law against Violence towards Women and the Family in Venezuela (the only Andean country without a VAW law until then), and the adoption of the legal procedures for implementing the existing VAW legislation in Bolivia, to the VAW campaign.

Some countries in Latin America and the Caribbean were more enthusiastic than others about the VAW campaign, as evidenced by the activities reported by UNDP, UNIFEM and UNFPA field offices for each country.[19] Box 9 outlines the campaign activities that took place in another Andean country, Ecuador, an example of a particularly comprehensive campaign.

The importance of research for campaigning

As noted earlier, Latin American NGOs consider research to be an essential part of their development activities, and the UN has often been an important sponsor of research. In Peru, Flora Tristan participated in the 'Multi-Centre Study on Sexual and Physical Violence Against Women', funded by the World Health Organization (WHO). Their two partners in the study were the Cayetano Heredia Peruvian University (Universidad Peruana Cayetano Heredia) and the Andean Centre for Education and Training Jose María Arguedas (Centro Andino de Educación y Promoción Jose Maria Arguedas), which is based in Cusco. In 2000, the three organizations interviewed a sample of 3351 women aged between 15 and 49 from Lima and the department of Cusco, covering issues such as the incidence of domestic violence, the injuries sustained by women, physical violence during pregnancy, child abuse, women's own attitudes towards violence, and gender roles, impacts and ways of confronting violence. The results were posted on their website.[20]

Other important research activities conducted by Latin American NGOs have focused on men's attitudes towards violence. The Peruvian NGO DEMUS, for example, interviewed eight male prisoners accused of rape, in a study published in 1995 (León and Stahr, 1995). The study comprised edited transcripts of the interviews, with evocative passages introducing the interviewee and the context of the interview, and comments on the interview material by a psychoanalyst and from a round table discussion. Apart from the illuminating analysis of the individual cases, what is interesting about this project is the use of a methodology characteristic of Latin American feminist research with women, namely the subject's personal story told in their own words, but this time the stories were the men's. Although, or perhaps because, the results are somewhat inconclusive, the method works well. The presentation of the material in this way gives a real sense of the individual stories and characters, as well as of the inconsistencies of accounts presented as truth, for most of the interviewees vigorously protest their innocence.

Puntos de Encuentro, Nicaragua, has conducted similar research into male attitudes towards male violence, allying it to their campaigning objectives. An interview-based research programme begun in 1997 was constructed with two aims in mind: to provide material for educational campaigns and to construct a methodology for practical work with men. They combined the production of a book with a series of magazine articles, public presentations, and radio and TV interviews. They also ran three workshops on masculinity in the same year, which enabled them to identify male leaders who could disseminate the discussions within their communities. As is often the case, Puntos' individual work

Box 9   The UN-sponsored VAW campaign

The example of Ecuador:

Preparatory work/reports

- Inter-agency activities centred on four key dates: 8 March, 5 June, 25 November and 10 December; coordinating several media activities.
- UNDP led a meeting with NGOs and other partners working in the area of violence against women to design and discuss gender violence and preparation of national reports on the subject.

Media

- A contest for radio spots on human rights was launched, with a distribution of prizes in Quito.
- TV and radio spots were produced and broadcast with national media.
- Essay, photo and drawing competitions were held, followed by separate expos of the best entries in the context of women's human rights.
- Newspapers ran stories: *El Comercio*, editorial section of *Society*, articles in *Expreso*, *Diario Hoy*, *El Universo* (11, 13 and 17 March).
- Television: the resident coordinator and a UNIFEM representative were interviewed by Iskra Calderón on Teleamazonas for a special report on gender violence to launch the Campaign (13 March); in Ecuavisa, Dagmar Thiel interviewed the spokespersons for the Campaign.
- Radio: the resident coordinator was interviewed in La Clave (12 March) and on HCJB, as well as in Radio La Luna and Radio Colon, COMPARTIENDO. Monica Muñoz of UNIFEM was interviewed on HCJB (18 March).
- In the context of World Population Day activities, UNFPA and UNIFEM helped to disseminate information through the media about the campaign for women's rights.

Training

- Women's human rights were introduced in the curriculum of the law faculty, in particular starting in Guayaquil.
- The project on Human Rights and Citizenship in Ecuador was established.
- In the context of two projects UNFPA supports in Cuenca and Quito, two workshops were organized to discuss strategies for

prevention and treatment of cases of gender and domestic violence, with a focus on the health system. The aim was to sensitize health providers to help prevent violence and care for women who have suffered from it. 'Gender, Health and Violence' was published to capture the main recommendations. Another outcome was a proposal to register cases of violence in health services.

Legal reform

- As follow-up to the approval of the Law Against Domestic Violence, and in collaboration with women's groups, UNFPA supported the National Council on Women and the congressional Special Commission on Women, Children and the Family to present a proposal for incorporating reforms in the Penal Code. The Penal Code that addresses cases of rape, incest, prostitution of minors and sexual harassment, had not been modified since 1971. The proposals included: deleting subjective terminology, such as referring to 'honest women'; increasing penalties for rape from two to four years; increasing the age of protection to minors from 12 to 14 years of age; defining and punishing sexual harassment, with incarceration of six months to two years; penalizing child prostitution.
- A number of seminars on women's human rights were held with lawyers and judges.
- UNFPA and WHO supported women's groups and parliamentarians in preparing proposals to incorporate sexual and reproductive rights in the 1997 Constitutional Reforms. The Constitutional Reforms recognize the right to personal integrity and forbid all forms of physical, psychological and sexual violence, and moral coercion.
- Through the initiative of the Municipality of Quito, and with the participation of various NGOs, a Network for the Prevention of Gender Violence was established with the participation of the Municipality, NGOs, UNFPA, UNICEF and WHO.

Public awareness campaign items

- Providing snacks to school children with the campaign slogan 'A Life Free of Violence: It's Our Right' written on each package.
- Other activities were the distribution of campaign products (posters, capacity-building kits, pens, stickers, pins, buttons, media kit, etc.), round table discussions, photo and essay competition, and news articles, etc.

From: www.undp.org/rblac/gender/natcamp.htm

on masculinity was combined with networking activities, in this case participation in the 'Men's Group against Violence' in Managua. This example of networking links back to the UN, which promoted the Nicaraguan group alongside groups from Mexico and the Canadian White Ribbon Campaign, in the VAW campaign of 1997–99. The UN also co-sponsored a meeting held by a group of social scientists at FLACSO (Facultad Latinoamericana de Ciencias Sociales, Faculty of Latin American Social Sciences) in June 1998 in Santiago, Chile. Its aim was to 'reflect on the accepted concepts of masculinity that impoverish the lives of men and are oppressive to women, and to take theoretical steps towards a new paradigm'.[21]

In Latin America, debates about masculinity and violence are still incipient, but crucial nonetheless, especially in countries such as Nicaragua and Peru, which have been marked by extreme civil violence, sometimes war, over recent decades. An understanding of the socio-historical context is important for effective work with violent men, a point recognized by a small number of projects worldwide. For example, Sally Engle Merry describes projects for male abusers in Hawaii and New Zealand, which situated violence against women in the context of the men's experiences of displacement, racism and degradation, and, without condoning the violence, linked men's anger and pain at such experiences to the way they treated 'their' women (Merry, 2001: 49). In Latin America, too, NGOs are beginning to explore different methods of working practically with men to address violence in both the personal and public domains.

Practical and personal work

This chapter has outlined the involvement of NGOs in rights-based training work and work on a personal level, much of which has coalesced around the issue of VAW. The example of the Gregoria Apaza Women's Centre shows how NGOs manage to integrate rights and empowerment approaches throughout their activities. The Gregorias have a three-pronged approach, which has been described as follows:

Integral intervention is carried out within a framework of human rights and an intercultural focus, through three programmes, each aimed at an area for empowering women:

- Local Advocacy ⇒ sociopolitical empowerment ⇒ training and guidance for women's leadership
- Technical Business Training ⇒ economic empowerment ⇒ training and consultation for women to become small business owners

- Personal–Family Enhancement ⇒ personal–family empowerment ⇒ addressing and preventing domestic violence

(Beltrán Sánchez, 2001)

For other examples of the Gregorias' work, see Boxes 1 and 4 in Chapter 4.

The final example, more specifically focused on VAW, is clearly linked to the processes of young and adult women assuming ownership of their rights. In the words of Mónica Beltrán Sánchez, 'beginning with information on their basic rights, on legal proceedings (legal literacy), and on enhancing their self-esteem, with information on alternatives they can choose in order to resolve their current or potential situation of violence (Beltrán Sánchez, 2001: 5). They have a wide-ranging educational programme, directed at women, public officials and outreach workers. Their legal literacy education for women uses materials on human rights and sexual and reproductive rights, including topics such as divorce and separation, the family code and the law on intra-family violence. Their educational materials for the outreach workers they train cover themes such as gender, sexuality, leadership, human and citizenship rights, conciliation and project elaboration, as well as the legal issues mentioned above. Meanwhile, they provide legal services and psychological counselling for victims of domestic violence.

Looking 'upwards', the Gregorias also operate at a city-wide level, becoming the first institution to preside over the Network for the Prevention of and Services for Domestic Violence in the city of El Alto, formed in September 1998. This network comprised a number of NGOs active in El Alto, the local Federation of Neighbourhood councils and governmental institutions, including the municipal government, the public health system and the police. In 2000, the Municipal Health Department took over the role of network facilitator. Among other achievements, the network produced training materials for neighbourhood councils and health personnel, ran training projects for the health sector, mobilized demonstrations for No Violence Day (25 November) and, perhaps most importantly, provided a forum for communication between member organizations and a means of channelling and documenting cases of domestic violence. Considerable difficulties remain, for example the persistence of cultural attitudes that consider domestic violence to be natural, the inadequacy of services and the rotation of personnel in public sector jobs. Nonetheless, the Gregorias consider it a positive experience which highlights the importance of inter-sector coordination in addressing the issue of VAW (Beltrán Sánchez, 2001).

Moving up another level, the Gregorias were a very important NGO partner for the UN campaign in Bolivia, for example producing the national report. They also participate in a number of Latin American women's networks.

What this extended example has shown is the way in which a rights-based focus requires NGOs to operate at varying levels. Research and advocacy are often combined with practical work on empowerment, self-esteem and legal service provision. Thus the individual woman is placed at the centre of a global legal system of rights instruments. The global elements of transnational networking represented by the UN influence NGO activities, not least because they provide financial support. However, it is important to remember that this process is not to be understood as purely 'top-down' – the UN campaign was itself inaugurated as a result of pressure from the women's movement at UN conferences and in regional forums.

Citizenship

We turn now to discuss what for many Latin American feminists was the 'next step' for the women's human rights campaigns of the 1990s. One of the most striking changes in the language of NGOs and a direct consequence of the spread of rights discourses in the region, has been the absorption of the concept of citizenship into their practice (Molyneux, 2000b). For example, in 1995, Flora Tristan identified its primary strategic objective as 'to contribute to the citizenship of women and to the recognition/exercise of their human rights' (Flora Tristan, 1995). The majority of the NGOs working with women and marginalized groups considered citizenship to be an important theme of their work. The links they made between citizenship, human rights and women's humanity were summed up by the influential Mexican feminist, Marcela Lagarde. Speaking at a workshop organized by Puntos de Encuentro in Nicaragua in October 1999, she said: 'women's citizenship is marked by the most important philosophical construction that we women have developed in this century, that is women's human rights. . . . Citizenship, as a way of democratic being, is the construction of women's humanity' (Lagarde, 2000: 15).

The normative Liberal definition of citizenship, as political and civil rights, narrowly understood as 'the right to vote and be elected', has been challenged by Latin American social movements and intellectuals who advance ideas of active citizenship, substantive citizenship and more radical interpretations of rights (Barbalet, 1988; CIDEM-REPEM, 1996; Hola and Portugal, 1997; López Jiménez, 1997; Palacios, 1997;

Bruch, 1998). As we have seen, for NGOs working with women, the regional preparations for the 1995 Fourth World Conference on Women in Beijing marked an important moment in the foregrounding of citizenship issues. In part as a result of the input from the Latin American women's movement, the Beijing Platform for Action placed special stress on the importance of full citizenship for women, highlighting a broad range of issues from political representation to violence against women. Citizenship continues to be a key theme for Latin American feminists. Marcela Lagarde argues, for instance, that:

> Citizenship is a . . . symbolic space in which we act in order to transform it and construct the minimum basis of a generic democracy. In order to be able to make all these changes, we women act in diverse spaces, but particularly in one . . . that is civil society. . . . Therefore, civil society and the state are two fundamental spaces of social and political participation where we need to think and articulate women's leadership (Lagarde, 2000: 16).

Box 10 details the views of two activists working with women's NGOs on the practical and theoretical implications of conceptualizing their work in terms of citizenship. They demonstrate the importance of context in setting priorities: highlighting for Bolivia the difficulties of assuming universalism and equality in an ethnically divided society, and for Peru stressing the importance of popular organization.

In general, NGOs felt that citizenship was useful as an evolving concept. It provoked discussion, was open to positive definitions and was politically opportune. Natalia, a programme director from a Bolivian women's NGO, felt it to be particularly useful because the idea of citizenship 'covers everything', by which she meant it spanned the public and private spheres. For a broad sector of NGOs in the region, citizenship was defined in terms of a spectrum of rights: social, economic, cultural rights, and the right to full political participation. The latter right was seen as a key element of citizenship for the activists we spoke to, most of whom explicitly widened the definition from formal electoral participation to participation at all levels of decision making in the community and society. Several NGO workers also pointed to the need to expand the meaning of other rights, such as civil rights to encompass security from violence on the streets and in the home, and others such as respect for difference in terms of culture, class and gender, autonomy and self-esteem, some of which had yet to be encoded in law. NGO workers in Bolivia and Peru who were involved in advocacy with or on behalf of indigenous women for access to good quality health treatment, stressed the need for quality service provision,

Box 10 Citizenship as advocacy concept

'Citizenship is a relatively new concept, I would say, which was first used at Beijing. Since then, the women's movement has been using the term, incorporating it into our activities. . . .With regard to my organization in particular, the idea of citizenship is connected to the work of some feminists in Paraguay. After the fall of Stroessner, various organizations (not just women's organizations, but pro-democracy ones in general) began to talk about citizenship – that is full citizenship, exercising rights and the restoration of democracy. Then, in the first preparatory conference for Beijing at Mar de Plata in 1994, there was a specific panel on women's citizenship. . . .

'Little by little we are realizing that although it is a Liberal concept, there are aspects which don't, in fact, have to be surrendered to the current trend of neoliberalism. Indeed, they can be perfectly well suited to the demands and needs of the Latin American population. I think that the main advantage is the fact that people can use this term to demand greater equality: from the most isolated indigenous person in Bolivian Amazonia, to the Andean peasant, to the middle classes in the cities, everyone can use this concept to make their demands. . . .

'Talking about citizenship implies talking about rights, about obligations, about a set of norms, and about recognizing a certain sort of institutionality. These are tools which our country is unfortunately only just starting to assemble; there is significant lawlessness here, there's a kind of silence when it comes to standards or norms, and no understanding of rights whatsoever. But the task in hand for us all is to give the word [i.e. "citizenship"] some content, and back it up with legal instruments, which the people can then use to *exercise* their citizenship.

'There are obstacles of course, and these would include the fragility of Bolivian democracy . . . and all the issues of race and ethnicity that there are here. We have to work hard on everything to do with difference. Yes, the new Constitution [from 1994] recognizes our status as a pluriethnic, multicultural nation, but there is no over-all acceptance or understanding of this on the part of the population. There are still many issues that are not yet properly dealt with in the Constitution. There is still racism in our society.

'Working with rights also has to do with how people appropriate those rights – if they don't even know that they have rights, then they're not going to be able to exercise them, are they? . . . I think the biggest difficulty for us is a general ignorance of what counts as citizenship rights and obligations. And this is where we really have our work cut out for us. But beyond that we have to strengthen people's sense of personal dignity, their self-esteem. At the end of the day, you aren't less of a person just because you are a '*cholo*'[22] or Indian.

Instead, you have to learn to fight your corner; and if people treat you badly, you must object and not just give in.

'The situation is probably much worse in this country – and countries like Peru or Ecuador with large indigenous populations – than it is in other countries, such as those of the Southern Cone, where they don't face the same issues as multicultural, multilingual countries. And, of course, they are much richer, with more equal distributions of income levels. . . . Certainly, another limitation for us is a structural one – poverty; the state of extreme poverty in which our country is living.'

Diana Urioste, Director of the Women's Network in Bolivia

'There isn't a well-defined sense of citizenship here in the broader sense of the individual's potential to take an active role in society, and the idea of believing that what affects your life could affect the lives of others. The collective side of this concept has been lost, I believe. Paradoxically perhaps, during the earlier terrorist years [i.e. during the Sendero Luminoso conflict] we were really strong: women were organizing themselves, poorer women too; and I think that such organizing gave us a sense of "I can intervene", "I can participate", "I can decide", which is how I see citizenship.

'For example, in the days of the collective kitchens, there was a law that affected all state food programmes. They wanted to put all state food programmes into a system, so that food would be made available on a restricted basis, only to women with a specified number of children, or with physical disabilities, and so on. We debated this with the women of the poor neighbourhoods and managed eventually to get the law changed so that control of the system would be in the hands of the neighbourhood women's organizations. Things like this gave us a sense of belonging, of citizenship and achievement, which was subsequently lost. Now, what there was by way of women's organizations connected to the collective kitchens has finally been decapitated. Everything related to the distribution of resources has become clientelistic, with the state in control; this implies a completely different relationship, which has just taken away any sense of citizenship.

'As for rights – I find it worrying to talk about rights in the abstract, or purely legal terms. I think you can't talk about citizenship without talking about organizing. Organizing is not something that is valued these days. In fact, there are even those who oppose the idea of collective organization. Of course, this is about opposing the idea of the dispossessed organizing themselves; after all, the business sectors are organized, so are exporters, in fact they have a very strong lobby, they are very powerful. . . .

'But by the end of the terrorist era, organized groups among the poor had been destroyed, they killed the leaders and they destroyed the means of organization at a popular level.'

Ursula Paredes, academic and feminist activist in Lima, Peru including non-discrimination on account of poverty, as an important element of citizenship. Flora Tristan, Peru and TAHIPAMU, Bolivia, found it necessary and helpful to produce leaflets informing indigenous female health service users of their rights. Indigenous women were all too often subjected to authoritarian health practices, which could result in unwanted interventions such as sterilization. The administrator of Flora Tristan's project in this area linked such work to self-esteem and empowerment. She emphasized how important the transition was in the language of indigenous female users of health services: from complaining that 'they are treating me badly' to 'they are discriminating against me' marks a crucial step not only in refusing to accept such treatment but in challenging it as illegitimate. In practice then, citizenship is deployed as a grounded strategic concept within a framework of discourses of empowerment, rights and participation, as further demonstrated in the example in Box 11.

The personal significance of citizenship: empowerment redefined

As is clear from the preceding sections, a crucial theme that emerged in discussions with Latin American NGOs, is the importance they placed on the personal and day-to-day meanings of rights for the people to whom development assistance is targeted. An integral part of their work with concepts of citizenship and of human rights more generally, is the importance of assuming the implications of rights on a personal level, as people acquire an awareness of their status as rights-bearing subjects.

Ana summed up one of the challenges facing her work with Bolivian women and citizenship thus:

> We have to demystify the idea [of citizenship]. It is very much managed by lawyers, that is to say, it is a very legal concept . . . and seems empty of content. We have to fill it with content, bring it down from 'above' and put it 'here'.

Redefining citizenship by placing the individual subject at the heart of the debate builds on earlier practices of Latin American social movements and on the continent's political culture more generally. Mid-20th-century legislation in Latin America that instigated universal voting rights and programmes such as universal primary education followed a Liberal integrationist agenda, responding to demands for inclusion in the established political system. More recent Latin American citizenship claims demand 'the right to participate in the very definition of that system, to define what we want to be members of' (Dagnino, 1998: 51).

Box 11 Learning citizenship

TAREA developed a programme of citizenship education for Peruvian schools. The course materials for schoolchildren were based on two main themes: gender relations and respect for cultural and ethnic differences. The materials for teachers emphasize living well with others. The exercise book, *What do we mean by citizenship education?* (Palacios, 1997), distinguished the different meanings of citizenship as follows:

- Citizenship as a juridico-political condition: of citizens of the nation of Peru recognized by the state as equal in rights, opportunities and obligations, independent of ethnicity, class or gender.
- Citizenship as a right and a responsibility to participate in the exercise of power.
- Citizenship as critical rationality and deliberation: not beginning or ending with the passing of laws, but expressing the aspiration that such laws be reasonable and possible for all citizens.
- Citizenship as coexistence with others.
- Citizenship as a choice: the importance of acting as a citizen, exercising rights and responsibilities.

The book aimed to encourage teachers to think about the above definitions and develop their own. In a section on the distinctiveness of citizenship in Peru, TAREA pointed to inequalities that inhibited the equal exercise of citizenship, drawing on the work of sociologist Sinesio Lopez (1997). However, their main focus was on how to educate people to act as citizens, and the book's status as a potential training material for teachers certainly inhibited its ability to be overly critical of the government. The implication was that if citizens exercised their own side of the bargain between community and state, the state would have to play its part.

The definition of a citizen offered is: 'The citizen is someone who feels him/herself free, belonging to a community of equals, and who searches voluntarily to give his/her opinion, to propose and decide about matters of common interest that would be *reasonable and possible* for all those belonging to his/her political community, committing him/herself and making him/herself responsible for change and transformation *in favour of equality and democracy.*'

This is in tension with definitions of citizenship which confine it to the formal legal relationship between the individual and the state, as membership of a national, political community enacted in the right to vote and be elected, and symbolized by passports or identity cards.

The debates over redefining citizenship are ongoing in Latin America, and NGOs have been active partners in discussions conducted at varying levels, through books, articles, workshops and campaign materials. But they are also engaged in practical work, as illustrated by a comment from Natalia:

> The theme of citizenship is not only about juridical citizenship or political citizenship. Rather, it is human rights, social citizenship, social rights, juridical rights and economic rights, such as consumer and vendor rights. Above all, I would say, it is a right of the individual, understood as the individual *in society*, in relation with others. So, the question of whether the state is more or less important, whether it is necessary for protecting citizens' rights or not, depends in the first instance on the citizen recognizing him/herself as such, as a citizen.

However, she argued, 'some NGOs have to convert ourselves into facilitating vehicles for the exercising of citizenship rights', but it was clear that she saw this as not only a matter of facilitating access to the political and legal systems. For most NGOs, citizenship as the right to have rights was also about being considered a person and, crucially, about *considering oneself* a person. In the opinion of Amy, a senior Peruvian project worker, 'We can begin to amplify citizenship processes only through the development of a consciousness of being a person with the capacity to make demands.'

NGOs considered that helping to create *active citizens* was a vital part of their work. It was essential in advancing the social changes that they were committed to realizing, and it was not confined to the public sphere. Luisa, a Peruvian programme director, asked:

> How can we talk of being a subject with rights, or of exercising our rights if we do not have the subjective basis of citizenship like self-esteem, autonomy or personal security? . . . Citizenship is defined in the public sphere, yes, but even if you consider it limited to the relationship between citizens and state, it is born in private life.

Through this work, NGOs positioned themselves alongside social movements that are redefining citizenship in Latin America. They viewed their role as one that spanned all levels of what might be called citizenship action, from the personal and private, through to international networks and UN conferences. Conceptualizing their development work in terms of rights helped them to develop programmes for change. At the heart of such strategizing was a philosophical orientation towards the idea of citizenship. A workshop on the theme of citizenship facilitated by CADEM for an indigenous women's group developed the following definition of 'citizenship culture', summed up by Eva, a workshop facilitator for CADEM, in Mexico:

It's a culture of the human being, irrespective of whether you are a man or a women, it is where you have possibilities to develop yourself – in your family, in your community, and in your country. [Citizenship culture thrives] ... where you have information of what is happening in your country; where you have the opportunity to participate in decisions that are taken in your community and in your country. For us, this begins in the family.

6 Meeting challenges: problems with rights

DESPITE BROADLY POSITIVE ASSESSMENTS, NGOs that were committed to integrating rights-based approaches into their work not surprisingly also signalled a range of difficulties in translating them into practical action. Some of the reservations that were voiced accorded with those that have been expressed more widely. Opinion has been divided in the scholarly, legal and development literature over the generalizability and desirability of rights-based development in an ongoing debate involving both practical and ethical concerns. This is not the place to rehearse these broader debates; instead we will focus here on the views expressed by NGO practitioners who identified several kinds of problems, which we have characterized as structural, cultural and ethical.

Structural obstacles

As discussed in Chapter 1, a number of our informants considered poverty to be the crucial structural obstacle to rights-based development, along with the material and financial shortages faced by many development agencies. In addition, the structural constraints that NGOs most consistently pointed to were associated with state or institutional failure. Principal among these were an adverse political culture, with particular reference to corruption, inefficiency and party/factional politicization, as well as what many felt was a lack of political will to support rights work. Many complained that their governments did not adequately enforce existing legislation and lacked economic resources, as well as suffering from a lack of continuity in personnel resulting from changes in administration as well as within the administrative structure.

In democratic contexts, as the issue of violence against women illustrates, legislation can serve to change public attitudes, as well as indicating shifts in public opinion and political will. However, the question for most NGOs is whether it can be enforced, and structural factors are clearly central to this. For example, informants from Nicaragua pointed to the lack of reach of the state in rural areas as a severe limitation to their work with rights: where people have to travel for days to access a judge, and where legal actions are costly, processing legal claims is difficult, regardless of the quality of the legislation. Problems of access are not confined to Nicaragua. A substantial proportion of the populations of Peru, Mexico and Bolivia suffer similar problems. Moreover the judicial systems of all four countries have, over the years, been prone to corruption and inefficiency. The problem of access to justice of poor and marginalized populations has been recognized by many donor agencies as an important area for their work, although much remains to be done in this regard (DFID, 2000c; World Bank, 2001).

As discussed in Chapter 2, these problems varied in scale, but in highlighting general institutional failure – be this in the political or judicial machinery – some NGOs felt that rights-based work might seem futile in the absence of broader programmes of institutional reform and a greater consistency in the application of legal norms. As Fernando put it:

> You can't defend human rights when laws just don't apply to the powerful, but only to the poor . . . when powerful people permanently infringe laws without punishment, human rights seems to some people a waste of time. So we have to struggle continuously against corruption and impunity.

The countries in this study suffer more or less severe 'democratic deficits', despite periodic anti-corruption efforts by politicians and the good governance programmes supported by donor agencies. While these programmes were welcomed and provided some leverage for reform processes, progress was slow. Rights approaches that relied on the effective operation of the legal system therefore met serious limits in this context. Party political control over the state bureaucracy could also serve as an obstacle to policy-based and legislative reform. The previous chapters have discussed some of the ways NGOs have found to get round these problems, and to interact constructively with the state despite their considerable reservations.

NGO–state relations

Not surprisingly, given these conditions, NGO workers felt that relations with government were difficult and unresolved, and many were unhappy with what they felt were their greatly expanded responsibilities. Others were more worried about donors giving national governments a greater role in managing NGO work, when these were far from well intentioned or efficient agencies.

NGOs in Latin America have long been involved in a debate about their changing role and functions, and have often expressed concern that they were becoming or could become para-statal organizations, effectively replacing the state in some domains, or serving as instruments or agencies of the state. While many donors urge greater cooperation with state agencies, fears were expressed by our respondents that this could, among other things, lead to their losing both their innovatory, challenging character and their ability to represent the demands of those groups within civil society that they were meant to serve.

These concerns have important implications for development assistance. The stress is increasingly placed by aid agencies and governments on the need to develop forms of 'partnership' between civil society and the state, to avoid the problem of poor coordination and fragmented service delivery. State–NGO relations under optimal conditions can work well and produce a healthy synergy. However, as evident from the reservations noted above, there are reasons to question the desirability of such relations. Civil society's proper role might best be seen as one that challenges and critiques the state, developing alternative approaches and more radical solutions to social problems than those normally offered by states (Fowler, 2000).

Many of the most innovatory and successful NGOs in Latin America, such as those discussed here, have emerged from social movements – sometimes in opposition to states – and many activists argue that this critical and independent role can be productive. This was felt particularly strongly by NGOs that emerged from women's movements. Under the increasing influence of feminist ideas, these had developed both a critical gender analysis of women's needs and specific ways of working that challenged prevailing patriarchal cultural norms. Women's NGOs have been among the most creative, using their analysis of gender relations to develop projects that tackle the multidimensional character of women's exclusion. Such approaches are often critical of government efforts, which are felt to focus on fulfilling certain narrowly defined policy goals. A Peruvian scholar illustrated this with the example of reproductive health: she thought that reproductive health had 'excessive resources' in comparison with other areas but was being narrowly linked to family planning or population control, rather than being viewed in a comprehensive way. Fertility control, in her view, should not be detached from issues of sexuality and female empowerment, and should be linked to education and employment if it is to be successful in both human terms and in terms of governments' demographic concerns.

From this perspective it is inconsistent to put development efforts into building civil society and then expect it merely to fulfil state agendas as a collaborative 'partner', in what has been termed a 'social contract' model of development. Alan Fowler argues that:

> employing partnership to create social contract arrangements everywhere will not be the most appropriate way of bringing about structural change from the perspective of poverty reduction. Contention is needed just as often as cooperation, if those who are poor and marginalized are to have any hope of being heard and really listened to outside of aid inducement (Fowler, 2000: 5).

Some informants felt that rights-based work has, for these reasons, renewed calls for NGOs to take a more independent stance from government, also reflecting a broader debate over whether rights work sustains the status quo or whether it can serve to advance more transformative goals such as deepening democracy and advancing social justice (Perry, 1996; Stammers, 1999; Evans, 2000). While critics of rights-based approaches were concerned that they promoted individualistic values and contributed to the process of desolidarization that has accompanied neoliberal development, some governments have worried that rights approaches could carry more political implications than conventional welfarist or developmental schemes. This latter view received some confirmation from the role that NGOs played in challenging the one-party rule of the Partido Revolucionario Institucional (PRI) in Mexico, and in Peru in criticizing Fujimori's abuses of power.

Development agencies must create definable and achievable objectives for their work, not least for reasons of upward accountability to the public. They need to be able to scale their work to certain manageable projects, which means that development work risks becoming more about administering finance than about supporting social change (Green, 2001). Some of the more innovative NGOs have an experimental side that enables them to create new methods of intervention, which they describe and refine through processes such as funding applications, evaluations and academic research. Rather than simply carrying out the wishes of the state or development agency, political activism and criticism (constructive or not) from NGOs or other organizations thus contributes to ongoing debate over policy. As noted earlier, the NGOs we researched believed that rights-based work did have transformative potential. Some thought that the human rights agenda revitalized an NGO sector that had lost its way in the 1980s. Fernando, a Bolivian network coordinator, elaborated:

> We are all questioning why we exist as institutions, as NGOs in Bolivia. After the 1980s debt crisis we lost our momentum. A large number of institutions became instruments of the state, or intermediaries between the state and civil society. So they did (and some still do) construction, social services, health, education – everything – and they lost their political element and their commitment to strengthening civil society and social movements, and to making demands for more participatory democracy and sustainable development. We therefore lost this focus, but the new agenda linking human rights to development has given us the opportunity to relocate ourselves within the social and political scenarios in Bolivia, and to rediscover our function of giving expression to the needs of civil society rather than to the needs of the state.

Professionalization

NGOs were, however, worried by the changes that had taken place in their own organizations and practice in response to the reconfiguration of state–NGO relations and donor pressure on them to professionalize. Some considered that this risked alienating them from their constituencies and in turn threatened to undermine their capacity for innovation and their sense of themselves as part of a political and social movement.

This fear explains the emphasis placed by Latin America women's organizations on maintaining autonomy from the state. Latin American women's movements have long been divided over the question of autonomy across a spectrum, with one extreme favouring entry into the state as functionaries and the other insisting on complete independence from it. The latter view, not surprisingly, prevailed until the process of democratization was under way, but the combination of the return to civilian rule and the new priorities of the international development agenda made working with the state both more possible and more necessary. Rights-based work and good governance agendas, in highlighting the need for legal reform and placing emphasis on advocacy work, brought NGOs into closer engagement with governments. Women's departments and policy units worked closely with NGOs in many countries, with the latter often playing a key role in the drafting of new laws and the provision of new services, effectively aiming to mainstream the demands and concerns of their constituencies.

For some activists, working with ministries and government agencies such as police departments remains a contentious issue. Many were alert to the dangers of 'cosying up' to the state and instanced cases of cooptation where civil society organizations ceased to represent the interests of their constituencies and became simply an arm of the state. A concern often expressed by activists was whether the Latin American women's movement had become overly bureaucratized. As feminist activists moved into state institutions, the movement itself became more 'NGO-ized' (Alvarez, 1998), losing some of its activist and arguably its representative character. This then is the underlying issue that divides the *políticas* and *autonomas* (i.e. those who engage in political institutions and those who remain outside of them) within the women's movement. Whether organizations consider that they work in, or against, or independently of the state, there is a fear that any loss of autonomy results in the organization becoming less effective.

Silvia, an experienced Bolivian feminist who has worked in both the NGO and state sectors, argued in favour of engaging with the state, but as part of a political movement rather than in a technocratic capacity:

> I think that this phenomenon of the bureaucratization of the women's movement has led to an approach that is too technical and not political enough. The feminists . . . have approached the state as technocrats, as functionaries, *asesoras* [facilitators], consultants, specialists and so on, but not as a political movement. You need a movement that negotiates a political agenda with the state, instead of entering through the back door.

She thought that a repoliticization of the women's movement would mean the difference between *exercising* rather than merely *proclaiming* rights.

For all these problems in the relationship between NGOs and governments, our respondents emphasized that it was not simply a question of whether or not to cooperate, as it was not a zero-sum equation of working exclusively in civil society or in government. Raquel, a Peruvian academic and activist, expressed a fairly widespread view that it was necessary to work in a variety of spaces:

> Achieving change happens through different approaches. The women's movement has different strategies and they all seem valid to me. Individual efforts don't change things, but collectively we move the debate along. It's not a case of either/or. . . .

Although of course you always have to be very reflexive when working with the state, and ask if you are really advancing things or if you are just keeping quiet because of a fear that the government won't accept your point of view.

The most important aspect of the women's movement was, in her view, the ability to propose positive ideas. This was a task that could be fulfilled from inside or outside the state. She believed that it was particularly important to be 'coherent', i.e. to have a clearly worked out programme and strategy, and to look for solutions rather than simply complain about the problems. Much, then, depends on the strategy of the women's movement itself, and how engaged in political and legal reform it is prepared and equipped to be. Much also depends on co-operation and coordination between the different parts of the movement, as Silvia explained:

The discussions about the law on violence against women were a very important meeting point between state and society, with activist women, the media and so on, and we had all the ingredients ready to create a new right for women. I was part of the government at the time and we asked activists to come to a meeting where the deputies were discussing the law. One told me they couldn't because they had to attend a workshop! ... And the most amazing example for me was when the parliamentarians were discussing the status of abortion in the new penal code; on that very day, most of the 'activist' women were away in Santa Cruz – in a workshop training them in advocacy and how to influence parliament.

Cultural constraints and ethical debates

The activists we interviewed saw prevailing cultural attitudes as the next most important limit on the kind of rights work they were engaged in. In addition to the factors already mentioned, as organizations concerned with both women's and indigenous rights they felt that discriminatory attitudes were a particularly important obstacle that they confronted.

Women's rights are especially prone to attack from defenders of the status quo on grounds of religion and tradition. Since dominant political cultures help to determine the rights that governments will selectively invoke, women's organizations in Latin America have sometimes found it difficult to campaign for women's equality, but even more so for sexual and reproductive rights. Demands for an extension of such rights face opposition from the Catholic Church and US aid policy. In contrast, as already noted, it was relatively easy to build a general consensus around violence against women, a campaign that gained the support of the churches and the conservative parties. However, such a campaign does not necessarily question gender relations and some activists felt it perpetuated a view of women as victims and stimulated paternalistic responses somewhat at odds with gender equality agendas. Raquel, for example, expressed her concern that this campaign only selectively addressed women's needs, and neglected what she saw as structural issues:

> Everything done around the issue of violence looks at the domestic level. It's true that the domestic level is one of the spaces of violence against women, but gender violence in public spaces just isn't dealt with . . . there is no analysis of gender violence at a social level, and there are no actions at a social level in relation to violence that has to do with public health, for example.

NGOs also came across forms of 'traditional' cultural resistance that are widely discussed in the literature on human rights that focuses on debates over cultural relativism (Dembour, 1996; Preis, 1996; Wilson, 1997; Esteva and Prakash, 1998). Several activists spoke of encountering cultural resistance to some aspects of rights-based strategies, where they came into conflict with customary laws and cultural practices. Rights work in such settings had to be pursued with sensitivity towards existing notions of justice, working with such conceptions where possible rather than against them. This was particularly mentioned by informants working with indigenous peoples in Bolivia and Mexico. Box 12 provides an example of an NGO grappling with just such issues.

Some interviewees referred to problems associated with working with abstract and theoretical legal notions of rights, some of which meant little when transposed to indigenous communities. However, both Latin American and British-based practitioners pointed out to us that, in their experience, if the concept of human rights is unfamiliar to, or resisted by, the people with whom they work, it is possible to find similar indigenous concepts and translate them into a language of human rights. For example, concepts of respect, dignity, justice and peace were all found to provide fruitful starting points from which to discuss the concept of rights. This approach implies an acceptance of a common basis within diverse cultures for such work, but it also reflects the degree to which the language and practice of human rights has become a global reality. Irrespective of cultural variations in the

Box 12   Working with cultural resistance

The Instituto de Servicios Legales e Investigación Jurídica (ISLI, Institute for Legal Services and Juridical Investigation) in Bolivia was involved in a consultative project that fed into proposals by the Ministry of Justice to develop legislation for the incorporation of customary law into the national judicial structures. They found that some Aymara communities enforce the death penalty for serious offences, contravening the right to life protected by the Universal Declaration of Human Rights and the Bolivian constitution. They spoke of the necessity for sensitivity, dialogue and compromise on both sides. For example, while they felt that the right to life should be seen as inviolable, detention in prisons, which is not a feature of community justice, can be seen as a form of corporal punishment. Prison may, in some circumstances, be less effective and more cruel than other community-based means of castigation which do not accord with Western definitions of appropriate punishment. They were optimistic about the possibilities for compromise on both sides: with 'Westernized' legislators understanding and respecting how indigenous justice works, and indigenous communities appreciating the protection afforded them by internationally agreed human rights such as the right to life.

applied meaning, human rights have become the *lingua franca* for marginalized groups all over the world, through which to make their demands of dominant groups. This global characteristic does not imply that the cultural norm of human rights is understood, negotiated or used in the same way everywhere (Dembour, 1996; Preis, 1996; Wilson, 1997; Cowan et al., 2001). Indeed, a recognition of the transversal character of rights, and of their adaptability to different contexts, is one of the reasons that human rights ideas have developed and progressed internationally since the 1940s. One of the contentions of this study is that such differences in understanding can and should enrich discussions of human rights in Europe and North America.

The cultural relativism versus universalism debate has become less polarized in recent years as the idea of culture as bounded and unchanging has lost conviction (Wilson, 1997; Cowan et al., 2001). If some donors erroneously assume cultural homogeneity within strictly defined ethnic groups, NGOs tend to have to work with far less clearly defined identity boundaries.[23] These shades of grey also operate in ostensibly straightforward legal issues, such as land rights (Whitehead, 2001). International donors have become increasingly committed to

encouraging customary legal arrangements, in the context of participatory development. However, this may not be the most equitable
strategy. Ann Whitehead argues that development agencies should be
prepared to encourage work for gender equity and change in both statutory and customary law, and stop viewing 'the customary' as either
more egalitarian than statutory law, or as homogenous, 'traditional' and
fixed, and therefore impossible to alter. She has shown that first, neither
statutory, Western systems of law nor, crucially, various local customary systems fully encourage gender equity in land-holding arrangements in Uganda; and second, that ordinary people use elements of both
systems to stake their claims, implying that the statutory and customary cannot easily be separated (Whitehead, 2001).

One of the main objectives of Latin American NGOs working with
women's rights was precisely to act on culture *in order to change it*, as
illustrated by the following quote from Maria, a director of a Bolivian
NGO.

> Not everything that is cultural is good. . . . 'Culture' is often used
> to justify violence and discrimination, not only against women,
> but also against other social groups that have been marginalized
> throughout history. If this is culture, it has to be changed.

This accords with much of the theoretical discussion of cultural relativism in human rights debates. Culture is itself dynamic, a point made
by Michael Freeman, who also argues that even if we accept that
human rights are a form of cultural imperialism, there are many
responses to imperialism, and it is arbitrary to take the most conservative as 'traditional' or representative (Freeman, 1995). Sally Engle
Merry also argues that it is erroneous to assume that either human rights
or 'culture' are unchanging, non-historical concepts, and that one of the
most important characteristics of *both* is precisely their dynamism.
Both are 'fluid, contested and changing entities', recognition of which
undermines the false opposition between human rights and culture
(Merry, 2001: 35). She argues that 'the important question of culture is
. . . how cultural practices [including ideas of human rights] are introduced, appropriated, deployed, reintroduced and redefined in a social
field of power over a historical period' (Merry, 2001: 46). This dynamic and reflexive view of rights is supported by the examples discussed
in this book.

Discussions of culture inevitably involve debates over individual
versus collective rights, and over the philosophical and ethical aspects
of working with rights-based strategies. One of the directions in which
human rights debates have moved is towards the increasing validation

of collective rights, a process that has been impelled largely by Southern governments and indigenous groups. The tension between individual and collective rights has been the subject of much debate (see Freeman, 1995), and was an issue that preoccupied a number of our informants. As the discussion of Nicaragua in Chapter 8 illustrates, human rights agendas were sometimes associated with the progress of an individualistic value system. Amy, a worker with a legal NGO in Peru, felt that there were also rights strategies that risked losing sight of the individual subject, and of their individual needs and interests, ones that are distinct from collective demands for sectoral rights. This has been especially important for women, who often find their individual rights at risk in communitarian, sectoral or nationalistic projects.

Collective sectoral demands not only risk essentialism, as occurs in the appeals to an unchanging eternal identity or culture, but more practically, they also risk fragmenting development lobbies, each working for one set of rights, such as women's rights, children's rights, the rights of indigenous peoples or rights to sexual preference. Silvia pointed out the advantages and disadvantages of working in this way:

> The advantages [of working with particularistic rights] have to do with visibility, and creating social actors. The recognition of our rights, as a gender, permits us to act with a social and political identity. . . . They have the advantage of 'potentializing', making visible, opening up spaces, but they are doing this in a context of other actors' severe weakness, of a very strong social fragmentation. . . . For example, women are gravely affected by poverty and problems that can't be resolved only through particularistic rights, but have to be resolved as policy, as social movement.

Furthermore, if the focus of human rights discourses becomes too closely associated with identity or sectoral politics, it risks marginalizing those who do not self-identify as purely or predominantly indigenous, black, female or young, etc. Often, those who do identify themselves using such categories similarly find that they have social personhood and recognized political agency only insofar as they are prepared to conform to external expectations of them. This is a particular problem for indigenous peoples, who, in making claims for their rights, often need to stress their 'traditional' sides at the expense of a nuanced portrayal of contemporary indigenous cultures (Ramos, 1998). In contrast, the category of 'the poor', despite its frequent appearance in World Bank, UN and DFID documents, lacks precise definition and meaning in the contemporary global context (Gledhill, 2001). Identity-based sectoral rights provide a framework to direct development and NGO assistance, but do not help those who fall between the cracks, and may indeed limit those who ostensibly fit the bill. One clear example of this is the focus of much development assistance to women on their reproductive role.[24]

However, the identification of such difficulties did not prevent our informants from, on the whole, presenting a positive vision of the potential of rights-based strategies. Most informants saw these problems as challenges, and as ways to orient and sensitize their work. In effect, the abstract theoretical debates indicated above are being tested in practice in a myriad of ways every day in the work of NGOs such as those in our study. Not only were they trying to resolve theoretical problems identified by others, but their work also contributes to the development of new theory.

7 Consequences: organizational implications of the shift to rights

WE NOW CONSIDER the organizational implications of incorporating rights into development practice. We argue that a number of institutional changes follow from the shift in the way that the subjects of development are perceived, i.e. from being seen as passive, needy recipients of aid, to active subjects of rights; from civil society as not merely a site of activity but an object of transformation; from culture as static and given, to dynamic and changeable; and from NGOs as deliverers of services, to participants in political and social transformations. Taken together they imply changing notions of NGOs' various forms of accountability.

In this chapter, we begin by focusing on upwards accountability, that is, NGO accountability towards (and relationship with) donors. Since we found that many of the tensions coalesced around evaluation procedures, we discuss indicators and potential and actual approaches to the evaluation of rights-based work. The theme of evaluation is continued through the latter part of the chapter, which focuses on downwards accountability, that is, the relationship between NGOs and their users. We assess the scope for increased strategic participation of users in NGO planning and evaluation processes, and argue that the recent increase in the participation of service users in evaluation processes has been a step forward for many NGOs. This is important for upwards accountability too, as evaluation should as a consequence be more rigorous and effective.

Changing visions of the subjects of development

As we have seen, a central aspect of the implementation of rights approaches developed by Latin American NGOs is a conceptualization of the subjects of development as active and central to development processes. In contrast with the passive subjects of 'charity' characteristic of traditional needs-based approaches (see Table 1, p.11) beneficiary participation is an integral part of rights-based development. Dorothy Rozga, from UNICEF, argues that 'from a human rights perspective poor people must be recognised as the key actors in their own development rather than as the beneficiaries of commodities and services provided by others' (Rozga, 2001: 7) This view has its precedent in participatory development, but the conceptual shift from 'charity' or welfare to rights implies a fundamental break with earlier approaches, in two main ways.

First, if development projects conceive of their users as subjects of rights, this means that they are recognized as having claims and entitlements not only against their national governments (or occasionally the international community), but also with respect to other development agencies, including the NGOs themselves. Many of the NGOs we consulted, both in England and in Latin America, have yet to see through all the consequences of that realization, but recent advances in their approach to evaluation indicate that steps are being taken in that direction. The increasing substitution of 'users' (or even 'citizens') for 'beneficiaries', combined with a greater focus on participation, has led to many NGOs seeking to include their users in their own decision-making processes.

Second, from the perspective of field-based practitioners, such shifts also imply a change in relations between donor and recipient NGOs. This involves a transfer of power to the recipient of development assistance, and a recognition of the fact that development is a shared political endeavour, in theory a genuine 'partnership'. From a rights perspective, NGO–donor and state–civil society partnerships should work both ways, with ideas and influence flowing from the bottom up as well as the top down. Such a partnership need not always be a co-operative relationship, as noted earlier. Indeed, rights approaches may mean that some NGOs take a more critical stance than some governments and donors would like, especially if their aims include social and political transformation, understood by our informants as more 'political' aims than those promoted by charity- or welfare-based approaches.

NGO–donor relationships

Although the shift in development priorities towards rights-based work has received a broad endorsement within the international community, responses from donors have varied. When asked if international donors had changed the focus of their discourse from charity to rights, Fernando, a network coordinator in Bolivia, was sceptical:

I think international organizations have changed their conception of what they should do, so we now have an anti-charity *discourse*. But I believe that in reality the words have changed more than action itself. For example, in Bolivia, 94% of health investment and 92% of investment in education comes from foreign credit or donations. This makes it charitable: it isn't sustainable,[25] so you cannot say that it is not charitable.

On the other hand, as we have seen, some of the NGOs in this study had received encouragement from donors to pursue all or some elements of rights-based work. One example of this is the steer from some donors to incorporate a gender focus in NGO work, which was appreciated by workers from the NGOs involved, as well as activists in the women's movement. As explained by Sonia:

The great majority of European NGOs are imposing a gender perspective on NGOs here, and I think it's a good thing. Of course, there was a lot of resistance at first, because most NGOs in Bolivia originated from the left, and the left in Bolivia and elsewhere in Latin America has always been very *machista* [male chauvinist]. But after a while, it became passive resistance and now people are conscious that if they don't incorporate gender into their work, they won't get the money for the project. So many are beginning to work with gender because they have been forced to, and they are also beginning to change their way of seeing reality.

However, there was wide variation in the relationships established with donors, and informants stressed that differences among donor agencies were also significant. Where possible, they chose their donors, looking for agencies they felt to be flexible and with whom they could have a genuine dialogue. Some NGOs were in a more privileged position than others in this respect, and were able to avoid those agencies that attempted to impose conditions they considered unfavourable. Sonia explained:

Donor agencies vary. In my organization we have worked predominantly with European NGOs, particularly Swiss, Dutch, English. . . . We hope to find people who think more or less along the same lines, and who will permit us to present proposals that let us go where we believe we should be going. . . . [We've] never approached the North Americans, because they have a different logic. The logic of efficiency is primary for them. I don't think it's bad, but things like solidarity and other values more related to human rights are more important to us. So we're selective, according to where *we* want to be and where we will feel supported in our work.

NGOs tended to favour donors who were prepared to commit to what they saw as 'political' projects, understood in this context as rights and citizenship work. The transformative nature of rights-based development interventions was a central theme of the interviews we conducted, and views about donor responses to this agenda were mixed. Some informants felt that there had been progress and that there were *more* openings for this kind of work, particularly with women. Linked to this was a greater emphasis on strategic impact rather than service provision. In contrast, others highlighted donor demands for resources to go directly to the target population in poverty reduction projects, which they felt was at odds with more long-term 'political' work. For example, donors did not always recognize the need for capacity building among those who make political decisions (such as congress deputies, senators or civil servants), since such work ostensibly lacked direct beneficiaries.

However, all our informants considered that donor agencies should be 'more courageous and more political', as they felt that such work could achieve a more lasting result. One Peruvian NGO worker even called for more direct political support and intervention from donor governments, in order to pressurize national governments on human rights and development issues. Some distinguished between Northern NGOs and governmental agencies. Silvia argued that the former were more able to act politically, and should conceive of their work in that light:

I think that international cooperation from NGOs – not bilateral agencies, which is different – must support the strengthening of civil society. They must be more political, and they must intervene less directly, focus less on such things as health services. Why? Because it is not sustainable. Moreover, we are entitled to expect the state to intervene in this area. As NGOs we cannot play the state's role. ... Civil societies in Latin America, in Africa, have to become stronger in order to strengthen public policies, to change our own democracies.

Thus, NGO perceptions of the shifts undergone by donors in favour of strategic action over service provision (rights versus 'charity') were varied, and the extent of donors' commitment to 'political' action was disputed and at times criticized for being insufficient. Where donors had shifted to demanding strategic impact, this was often justified by concerns for sustainability (i.e. the long-term prospects for project effectiveness without a reliance on external funding). Yet NGOs were worried that donor demands for greater sustainability could be a two-edged sword. On the one hand such demands were considered positive insofar as sustainability could be a way to escape from donor control over their activities. On the other hand many cautioned that if a health or education programme's sustainability was made dependent on user fees, for example, it could be put at risk, because the populations with which they work are very poor and unable to pay much, if at all, for their services. Service provision was not necessarily always a bad strategy, and in many circumstances they believed it was a valuable, even essential, part of meeting more democratic aims.

An important criticism concerned the administrative demands made by donors. These often inhibited NGO work. As Juana said, 'while you're producing the report, drafting the project, drafting the operation plan and undergoing evaluation, at what point do you actually do the work you should be doing?' Almost all agencies demand a report twice a year, each of which involves at least 15 days of work, and agencies often request reports in different formats. Since no NGO relies solely on one donor, this represents a great deal of work that is unrecognized and under-resourced. Many agencies also demand that their money be put in a separate bank account, creating further administration for the recipient NGO. Several informants pointed out that if the different agencies could agree on a common format for their reports, or would accept a report written according to the NGO's internal format, this would lessen the administrative burden for them. In other words, the common view expressed was that a balance between accountability and transparency, and overloading NGOs had not been achieved.

Many of the problems highlighted by interviewees resulted from the tendency to fund projects rather than organizations. Our informants identified only a few donors who were prepared to fund expenditure on non-project-based aspects, such as administration, their own institutional strengthening, fundraising expenses or documentary research. Such funding was also notoriously fragile, with some of the more institutionalized NGOs at risk of becoming 'victims of their own success' (Sarah Bradshaw, personal communication), where funders decide that they are functioning sustainably and that non-project-based financial support can be withdrawn. In addition, the propensity of large agencies to pigeonhole projects meant that creative projects with end objectives commensurate with the donors' but differently conceived, can 'fall between the gaps' of donor strategizing. For example, Puntos de Encuentro found it difficult to attract funds for working with young people (as opposed to children), and a large media project such as a proposed TV programme aimed at changing attitudes was not considered a social project; but neither was it income generation or traditionally educational. It therefore struggled to attract funding, although it was in this case ultimately successful, achieving funding from UNIFEM's Trust Fund in Support of Actions to Eliminate Violence against Women. Informants acknowledged that constraints on development agencies themselves sometimes led to a lack of flexibility, which in turn inhibits the emergence of new aims, objectives and forms of intervention. The Latin American NGOs we investigated responded to such limitations through creative presentation of their projects, while trying not to compromise their own integrity. They were proud of their role in creating new terrains for their work and methods of intervention, and pushing the development debates forward. For their part, those donor agencies with effective rights-based approaches do acknowledge the importance of NGO expertise and recognize that to develop this, the NGOs themselves require some measure of autonomy.

Evaluation

Central to our interviewees' assessments of rights-based approaches and their relationships with donors, was the theme of evaluation. NGO concerns about donors' administrative demands and the provision of technical assistance often focused on the vexed question of how to measure the achievement of rights-based objectives. For example, they found it difficult to measure what they considered to be the most crucial aspect of their work, namely people's abilities to *exercise* their rights. NGOs found it difficult to square these kinds of aims with the terms of the cost–benefit equation demanded by most donors.

In Latin America generally, the pressures in recent decades towards professionalization and greater accountability have meant that NGOs have increasingly had to involve themselves in discussions over more formal mechanisms for the evaluation of their work (Bejar and Oakley, 1995). Our informants were not averse to this. Indeed, a number of the NGOs we discuss were in the process of developing more formal monitoring and evaluation procedures at the time the research for this book was carried out. While no-one we interviewed disagreed with the principles of evaluation and accountability, all thought that there were major problems in developing successful evaluative procedures in relation to some of the work that they were doing and that they considered of great value. Some feared that evaluation methods proposed by donors in relation to development work with communities around rights issues failed to capture the essence of the work, putting it at risk from dissatisfied donors. They emphasized that a project's impact on people's self-esteem, sense of entitlement, organizational capacity or 'empowerment' is extremely difficult, if not impossible, to measure and the results may only become evident over time.

Processes of evaluation

Much of the recent NGO and academic literature on evaluation produced in Britain and elsewhere emphasizes the importance of developing good methods for evaluating projects. In recent years, this is an area that has developed a range of methodologies such as participatory rural appraisal (PRA), surveys, logical framework analysis and cost-effectiveness analysis. Authors put much stress on active stakeholder participation, including the NGO users (Feuerstein, 1986; Marsden and Oakley, 1990; Gosling and Edwards, 1995; Mansfield, 1997). David Mansfield (1997), writing for Save the Children, summarizes much current thinking in his recommendations for evaluation procedures:

● The assessment of impact and not just outputs, including unintended impacts.
● The active participation of all stakeholders, making evaluation integral to the whole project process.
● An appropriate balance between internal review and formal external evaluations.
● The feeding-in of evaluations to policy development.
● The use of participatory methodologies.

There is a large body of expertise available on methods for evaluation and many of these ideas are currently being applied within the Latin American context. In practical terms, and without exception, our informants had developed a clear notion of their long-term objectives (see Table 2).[26] The NGOs we discuss in this book were developing new processes and indicators to evaluate their progress towards these goals. To this end, many had established baseline data and indicators of their own, and used formal surveys and research to measure impact in terms of perceptions and attitudes. However, their principal method of evaluating their work was in fact through users' individual life stories. They also drew on external expertise, particularly that of impartial experts. Some said that they would like to develop longer-term evaluation procedures that involve users.

The evaluation of development activities is always a difficult task, but rights-based NGOs face specific challenges. The chief issues raised by our interviewees were the time evaluation took and the fact that adequate measures of success were not, or could not be, established. Informants believed that rights-based work was a long process. They argued that the evaluation of rights-based strategies should ideally be on a medium- to long-term basis, or at the very least should recognize the fact that tangible results cannot be expected in a short period of time. This was a point also raised at the consultative meeting we held with members of Northern NGOs. At the same time, if impacts are expected over ten or 15 years, it is then hard to distinguish the effect of particular projects, or even of particular organizations.

Over time, many other factors may come into play, including the political situation in the country and the changing economic circumstances, both of which have an effect on local communities, their expectations and their ability to make demands of the state or other actors. Crucially, several informants frankly acknowledged that *sometimes there was no discernible impact*, but they continued to believe in the validity of their work as an end in itself. Informants felt that donors requiring satisfaction with regard to verifiable impacts should place more trust in the expertise of their partner organizations and the users of those organizations, and believe in the value of good projects in and of themselves. This was seen by some as a logical consequence of the shifting nature of the donor–recipient relationship resulting from donor agencies' own adoption of rights approaches.

Indicators

Linked to the changing relationship between donors and NGOs was the issue of quantifiability. Many interviewees mentioned the difficulty of developing appropriate qualitative or quantitative indicators for assessing their rights-based work. A number of them criticized what they felt to be an excessive desire to quantify among donors, a common criticism of prevailing methods from within the development community more generally. The quantifiability of an impact does not make it inherently more desirable. For example, just because income generation is measurable quantitatively, it does not prove that economic gain is a more valid goal than the less easily measurable goals of empowerment, increased self-esteem or creativity. Where donor agencies were exploring more qualitative methods of evaluation, and providing technical assistance in that area, our interviewees were enthusiastic. A number mentioned Save the Children UK and Canada as particularly effective in this regard.

One approach to the question of developing useful indicators and characterizing impact is in terms of social development, which Rahman (1993) has defined in terms of the following criteria:

- qualitative elements of empowerment, such as social awareness and self-reliance (defined as the combination of material and mental strength by which one can deal with others as an equal)
- elements of organic development, such as development of creativity, organic knowledge rooted in people's lives
- social development of the wider society: human dignity, popular democracy and cultural diversity.

Clearly, such criteria, like those of wellbeing, are not easily translated into measurement indicators, but they represent principles which remain important yardsticks in assessing such work. Rahman is at pains to stress the importance of empowering people themselves to articulate and assert their own feelings and develop a subjective set of indicators.

Latin American NGOs draw on such principles in their attempts to define indicators that could be of use to them in evaluating their work. They are not alone: an Oxfam report of 1997 mentions the need for the development of generic indicators for measuring impacts on gender relations and women, as well as for the impact of capacity building in health, particularly community-wide (Yanni, 1997). However, it is not an easy task. Just as indicators designed with only the project objectives in mind may miss unintended impacts, good or bad (Mansfield 1997), indicators focused only on the subjective experience of either users or NGO workers may also give a partial picture of the impact of the project. Our informants felt the need for some key questions to be developed which could form the basis for helping NGOs to analyse both the impacts and the objectives of their rights-based work; while triangulation techniques involving third-party assessments would balance out the subjective experiences of both NGO workers and users.

Despite these difficulties, NGOs were developing considerable expertise in the design of evaluation and monitoring systems, including appropriate indicators. Our interviewees suggested some criteria they thought useful, which are presented in Box 13. These are intended to complement indicators more specifically tied to broader objectives (such as the achievement of economic independence). It is important to stress that evaluative criteria can never, in their entirety, be consistently appropriate to different contexts and consequently should not be treated as prescriptive. There is clearly a need for further comparative research aimed at expanding this through a global investigation of NGO experiences in developing such indicators.

Box 13   Indicators for evaluating rights-based projects

Quantitative indicators

- Attendance at NGO events and use of NGO services; positive feedback from users.
- Profile of NGO in the community: numbers of people who have heard of it and value its work.
- Numbers of those who have come into contact with NGO materials or course ideas (as in the example of numbers of people trained by legal or health promoters) – the multiplier effect.
- Numbers of people in target group (including those who have attended the NGO and those who haven't, as an indication of general societal change) in public decision-making positions.
- Level of demand for courses or services.
- Number of new organizations resulting from NGO work.
- Reduction in incidence of domestic violence in the community. This is not just relevant for women's NGOs, but might provide an indicator of the nature of gender relations more generally.

Qualitative indicators – participant response

- Use of NGO work/ideas in daily lives.
- More confidence, self-esteem, greater capacity for negotiation and non-violent conflict resolution.
- Perceived ability to make demands of the state.
- User enthusiasm for NGO work/ideas.
- Awareness of sociopolitical context.
- Subjective perceptions of change in their lives and of the role of the NGO in this.

Qualitative indicators – societal response

- Policy or legislative change.
- External respect for NGO: among target community, media, national government (international presence can be relevant).
- Awareness in the media of rights/legislation.
- Involvement of social movements in promoting positive change.
- Development of pressure groups and new institutions, or helping to support such development.
- Politicization of target group generally (not just users of NGO).[27]
- Change in attitudes within political parties, government, social movements, development NGOs, civil society generally.
- Position of rights-based elements within existing development initiatives at NGO or governmental level – amount of influence.

Evaluation approaches

Beyond general indicators, NGOs were developing their own evaluative processes sensitive to their local context and individual objectives and capabilities. The next two boxes provide examples of this, as illustrations of good practice. Box 14 explores the evaluation processes of one educational organization in Peru, while Box 15 is drawn from one of the organizations examined in further detail in Chapter 8.

Downwards accountability and user participation

NGOs' criticisms of donors' evaluation and administrative demands can be read as their view of where their own accountability was directed and where it should be directed. Changing notions of accountability are a crucial aspect of the changes promoted by rights-based visions of development. As Caroline Moser and Andy Norton point out, some donors are beginning to recognize this, through measures such as:

> Developing new forms of accountability that enable NGOs to pursue their own objectives and work towards increasing the accountability of governments to civil society, rather than only ensuring the accountability of NGOs and CSOs to donors. Such forms of accountability focus on minimum forms of financial accountability and NGO identified indicators of process and outcomes rather than delivery of donor specified outputs (Moser et al., 2001: 45).

The practitioners we interviewed were resisting the notion of an exclusive emphasis on upwards accountability to donors on the donors' own terms. They were trying to develop evaluation procedures that enhanced both upwards and downwards accountability. The latter was at an earlier stage. However, it would be fair to say that the adoption of rights-based approaches to development is beginning to lead to a reconfiguration of the relationships between those 'doing development' and those supposedly benefiting from development. The implications of these changes for the NGOs themselves are, as yet, not fully apparent or adequately explored.

As noted earlier, some changes in the relationship between users and NGOs is evident in the shifting terminology describing those to whom services are directed. Since the term 'beneficiaries' is today identified with welfarist connotations, and 'clients' implies that services are

---

Box 14   Evaluating education

Fomento de la Vida (FOVIDA) conducted two investigations of its school for women leaders of community organizations in 1995 and 1998. Both assessed the types of user of the organization and made recommendations for the following phase of work.

The report of 1995 (Robles and Ordoñez, 1996) was written by two external researchers. It investigated the user group, in terms of social position, the nature of leadership, their ways of learning and the types of knowledge they had. In this way, it functioned as baseline data for subsequent evaluations. It used survey interviews with a sample size of 370. The questionnaires were filled out in large or small group sessions or during individual visits. There were four questionnaires: socioeconomic data, a leadership profile, learning styles and capacity-building needs.

The second report (Cáceres Valdivia et al., 1998), which was more explicitly evaluative, was written by a team of one external researcher and two NGO workers in charge of the school. It was based on interview data, with a sample size of 50, and drew on earlier data from the previous report, as well as reports published by FOVIDA about the school. It investigated the user group's perceptions of changes in themselves, their own organization and the school itself. It also investigated perceptions of changes in the country, politically as well as socially, and concluded that 'a crucial aspect of the construction of leadership today in Peru has to do with the capacity to articulate diverse interests and to construct global understandings' (p. 81). The researchers found that about a third of their responses expressed just such a 'global vision of the country, the world, politics or economics' (p. 80). Thus, the politicization of their user group was seen as an important part of their work, and an indicator of success. By this, they meant that users should come to an awareness of their sociopolitical environment and political agency.

---

monetized, the term most often used by our informants was '*usuarios/ usuarias*', translated as 'users'. Interviewees spoke generally of the importance of having respectful relationships with the users of their NGOs. Two programme directors, in Bolivia and Peru, explicitly discussed their preference for using formal forms of address (*usted* instead of *tu*[28]). Most of the NGOs in this study were trying to address problems of paternalism in their work. Informants were well aware of the need to establish appropriate relationships of a democratic and egalitarian character within the remit of NGO work, something that has not always been the case in development projects. However, only a few

Box 15   Evaluation in practice

Puntos conducted an evaluation of the first five years of its work, in April–August 1996 (Arosteguí et al., 1996). This served as a basis for its strategic plan for 1997–2001, and was undertaken with this objective in mind. It involved external evaluators, who conducted fieldwork, interviewed key informants and evaluated the institution. They worked in collaboration with Puntos personnel, in defining indicators and elaborating methodological processes, hypotheses and conclusions. The evaluation consisted of three components:

- A survey of homes throughout Nicaragua, to evaluate the impact of Puntos' programmes and the levels of acceptance of Puntos' primary themes in public opinion.
- Interviews with 58 key informants.
- An external investigation of Puntos as an institution, drawing on documents, interviews with personnel and group work sessions. This was to measure the coherence in different understandings of its mission, strategies and programmes, as well as its efficiency and use of resources.

Puntos considered the evaluation to have been characterized by its holistic and participatory methodology. The group sessions also involved a transference of skills, as Puntos personnel took advantage of the opportunity to learn key elements of research, analysis and evaluation methods from the evaluators. The evaluators also taught statistical software programs, and explained their methodologies as time permitted. Furthermore, the information gleaned during the survey stage of the research was returned to the communities involved as quickly as possible. It thus became a mechanism of institutional accountability towards all those interested in the future of the organization.

thought that their organizations had changed significantly in this regard.

Such renegotiations in NGO–user relationships are clearly evident in the mechanisms used for accountability. We discuss these using the distinction between strategic and functional accountability made by Edwards and Hulme (1995), citing Jeffrey Avina (1993). Strategic accountability covers impacts on other organizations and the wider environment on a medium- to long-term basis. Functional accountability concerns the short-term monitoring of resources, resource use and

During the participatory exercises for this study, we asked how the workers would evaluate the impacts Puntos had achieved. Some of the responses follow.

Processes/methods

For the television and radio programmes:

- Review of audience letters, opinion surveys, focus groups.
- Analysis and monitoring of the content of communications media for prevalence of specific themes.
- Development of other media programmes with a similar focus.

For campaigns:

- Opinion surveys, attitude scales, in-depth interviews.
- Coverage of and demand for materials produced by Puntos.
- Coverage of the theme in the media.

Indicators

For a specific programme which dealt with changing men's attitudes:

- More women elected in political posts and decision-making positions.
- How fathers relate to their children, what aspirations they have for them.
- Men searching for information on relating to women in positions of equality, talking about the issue of gender equality, and making an effort to communicate with women at organizational and interpersonal levels.
- Lowering of rates of domestic violence and violence more generally.

immediate impact. We take 'downwards' functional accountability to refer to the evaluation of practice, with the aim of making the practice of the NGO relevant to the needs or demands of its users (rather than the donors); strategic accountability includes involvement or input into the strategic design and planning of the NGO.

Functional accountability to the users within the NGOs we investigated was based on three main mechanisms: research projects, and formal and informal evaluation procedures. User participation as research subjects was perhaps the main means of involvement for both service-based NGOs and those that provided technical support to other organizations. Some interviewees spoke of user participation as researchers. For example one human rights organization in Nicaragua was training women to research the effects of development projects in their areas. Certainly, research is an integral part of the design of projects for most Latin American NGOs, many of whom are uniquely placed to generate valuable data. Where our informants analysed the influence of internal factors on changes in their NGO, they tended to point to their own research projects or evaluations as important influences on their practice. Others spoke of academic research as one of their main types of work, although it was a priority for only one organization, TAHIPAMU in Bolivia. However, most felt they were in need of more support, both technical and financial, from donors for undertaking this kind of work. The development of research projects both reflects the trend towards the greater professionalization of NGOs and the effects of the relative paucity of local research into marginalized populations in Latin America during the late 1970s and early 1980s. NGOs conduct periodic research projects which often take the form of questionnaires and/or the collection of personal histories. They enable project leaders to decide to whom they should be directing their work, who is using their services and what are their demands and preoccupations. More than half of our informants spoke of developing or already having formal research-based follow-up and evaluation procedures on a fairly large scale.

Where NGOs engage in educational activities, our informants stressed that they had a methodology that sought to enhance user participation as active learners. They also tended to conduct formal evaluations of their courses and/or services in a more systematic and ongoing way. These could take the form of feedback sessions, typically using short questionnaires; for example, two classes that the authors attended distributed such questionnaires. However, although questionnaires can be an important source of evaluative information, they might not be entirely reliable, especially in terms of encouraging criticism of the courses. In both instances, the course participants were not given much time to reflect on their answers, and they filled them out in front of the course facilitator. They may therefore have been reluctant to express criticism. In addition, written questionnaires could be a problem where NGOs work with people who are uncomfortable with expressing themselves in writing. In response to our requests to course participants in a number of workshops for their thoughts on the course, we found a general reluctance to criticize. This is not surprising, but should not be taken to indicate wholesale approval of each course. Participants may feel that any project is better than nothing, and that they need time to be able to build up a relationship of trust with an impartial observer before voicing criticism. On the other hand, it was obvious to us that informal downwards accountability was substantial. If appropriate relationships are developed with users, dissatisfaction is expressed to the facilitators either directly, or in mumbled comments, lack of concentration and the like. Furthermore, if people find the courses or services irrelevant or badly delivered, they simply do not attend, and they discourage others from doing so. During courses and consultations, comments made by participants feed into the NGO's understanding of what are the most relevant and important issues for their users.

More formal qualitative and participatory mechanisms for functional accountability may include user committees, which have been established by, for example, Manuela Ramos in Peru. However, there is the problem that user groups and committees are not inherently or necessarily participatory. The level and quality of participation depends on a number of important factors, such as institutional structures and variable power relations. Furthermore, participation does not automatically lead to accountability; in a disabling environment, where communities do not have the capacity to exercise their rights and responsibilities, participation may mask rather than reveal a low level of accountability (Cornwall et al., 2000).

With regard to strategic accountability, only one informant, from Puntos de Encuentro in Nicaragua, mentioned that she would like to develop mechanisms for greater direct user participation in the design of her NGO's strategies. For most of the NGOs we examined, strategic accountability came from relatively passive participation in periodic large research projects, and the various formal and informal ways users had of expressing their views and concerns to course facilitators or legal advisers. This was especially effective for those NGOs that primarily provided educational services, since their constituency (usually those in leadership positions) were better educated, had greater self-confidence and managed the language of evaluation with greater proficiency than those in the most disadvantaged social groups. They were therefore more capable of controlling or at least influencing the development of the NGO's services. Those who provided technical support for other organizations thought there was a greater potential for strategic as well as functional accountability towards the user groups. These NGOs both proposed their own projects and responded to requests from civil organizations for assistance in certain areas. The organization(s) to whom NGOs provided a service were able to stop collaborating with the NGO when they felt its input to be either less relevant or less necessary. Indeed, the aim of a number of NGOs of this type was precisely to make themselves redundant in the long run. Since much of their work was collaborative, a longer-term symbiotic relationship often developed, which lasted beyond the life of individual projects.

Accountability and egalitarian relationships

While there are many different ways of enhancing downwards accountability, *transparency*, especially with regard to finances, is acknowledged to be crucial. This was an issue raised by a number of people outside the NGO sector in Bolivia, who spoke of instances of conflict between NGOs and some communities who felt that NGO funds should be coming more directly to them. As noted in the Introduction, many of the development initiatives on good governance have focused on state and commercial institutions, and on the role of corruption in obstructing accountability. However, several informal discussions during fieldwork showed that corruption, or perceived corruption, was also a problem for NGOs.

Dissatisfaction, even conflicts, can occur where NGOs are perceived to spend the majority of the money they receive on their own facilities and staff wages, rather than on those they are ostensibly helping. Yet, as one informant pointed out, NGOs need to attract professional people to work for them, which involves a level of income often very different to that of the people with whom they work. In addition, they need certain equipment to work efficiently and to comply with the requirements of their donors. She argued that this was an area in which a rights-based approach from donors and the international community could help. If the whole context of development understanding were to shift from the still-continuing view of NGOs as based largely on goodwill, to a proper recognition of their work and their professional needs, she felt that the potential for resentment could be reduced, especially if it was accompanied by procedures which allow for greater transparency and general accountability to the public.

Effective rights-based approaches thus imply more egalitarian and mutually respectful relationships between all the participants in development – users, NGOs and donors. This accords with democratic principles and extends to one further set of relationships, that is those between NGO workers themselves. One indicator of good practice within a rights-based NGO may be the degree to which a proclaimed egalitarian discourse is consistent with the practice of the organization itself.[29] Certainly, internal democracy has been a long-standing principle of feminist movements. However, in practice it is a complex and largely unresolved issue, and its presence or absence cannot be the sole criterion of assessment of rights-based work. Good work may be promoted from within hierarchical structures, and the development of *effective* workable mechanisms of internal democracy evolves over time. In general, the smaller NGOs in this study exhibited more internal democracy, while the larger ones with sizeable administrative structures were more hierarchical. However, size does not always preclude democracy, as the example of Puntos de Encuentro shows. This NGO has given much thought to internal democratic procedures, as we will see in the discussions of good practice in Chapter 8.

For NGOs in this study then, the centrality of the concept of participation in rights-based approaches to development has meant replacing the recipients of 'charity' with subjects of rights and placing people at the centre of development. For most, this has implied a serious rethinking of their work and the consequent reconfiguration of various relationships: state–citizen, state–civil society, NGOs–civil society, NGOs–users, workers within NGOs and NGOs–donors. Chapter 8 discusses two case studies to explore in greater depth some of the ways NGOs have set about promoting such reconfigurations.

8 Case studies

THE FIRST PART of this book examined the ways in which rights-based approaches to development work were understood by local experts, i.e. NGO workers. In this chapter, we present two case studies which show in more detail how particular NGOs have chosen to work with this approach and how the *local context* critically shapes the articulation and practice of rights-based approaches. The two organizations are committed to similar goals and practices, both work with women and have been in existence since the beginning of the 1990s. The first is an indigenous women's organization in a rural area of Mexico. The second, a Nicaraguan NGO, was based in Managua and worked predominantly with women, but also with young people on issues of sexuality and 'adultism'.[30] Both, therefore, had a gender focus, but put it into practice in different ways. While the Mexican organization was very happy to conceive of its work in terms of women's rights, the Nicaraguan NGO was somewhat resistant to describing itself as having an explicit rights-based approach, preferring instead to focus on the concept of autonomy.[31]

Both organizations illustrated in their practice one of the trends in NGO work that we have identified, namely that they see their primary role as supporting community processes of self-organization. For many of the NGOs of this type, this was the basis of their strategy for enabling marginalized people to claim and exercise their rights. These case studies illustrate this development. The Nicaraguan NGO situates itself squarely in a history of community organization seen as a value in itself; while the Mexican GRO is an example of an organization that split in two, with one part becoming an indigenous women's GRO and the other an NGO which provided support for them and other local community organizations. We suggest that the more independent relationships that have emerged between development workers (NGOs of this type) and development beneficiaries (community organizations) are indicative of a general shift in attitudes towards development activities. We have characterized this as a shift from a needs-based, 'charity' focus, to rights-based approaches that incorporate more emphasis on participation and empowerment.

Maseualsiuamej Mosenyolchikuanij, Mexico

Maseualsiuamej Mosenyolchikuanij (hereafter MM) had an explicit focus on poverty alleviation, but there were some key ways in which its organization, with an essential focus on needs, had shifted to what we would characterize as exemplary of rights-based practices. As a result of its status as a membership organization, MM was relatively participatory and democratic. However, of greater relevance is the history of MM's relationship with its non-indigenous facilitators.[32] They had initially been part of the GRO, and had effectively become its leaders, but in 1995 they separated from the GRO to form their own NGO. The latter was intended to provide support for MM and other community organizations in the region.

MM provides further evidence of a 'needs to rights' shift in the subjective experiences of progressive empowerment identified by some of its members. It would be inaccurate to suggest that this was experienced by all of its members, but a number of individuals felt personally empowered through their membership of MM. The organization itself also grew; initially it was solely devoted to selling women's craft work, but by the time of our research it supervised a number of projects, from small enterprises, community farming and health projects, to a hotel owned and run by 47 MM members.

Puntos de Encuentro, Nicaragua

Puntos de Encuentro provides an example of an NGO that has a commitment to principles of democracy and participation, and to enhancing the capacity of disadvantaged groups to secure a greater hold on resources. However, at the time of the research, the members of this NGO explicitly refused the label of 'rights' work, for a number of reasons. They felt that problems associated with rights discourses in the specific context of post-Sandinista Nicaragua made it difficult for them to conceive of their work in terms of human rights. This, combined with disillusionment with international processes, had led to them having a negative vision of human rights work. They preferred to work with and through the concept of 'autonomy'. Their approach nonetheless clearly differentiated them from needs- or welfare-based organizations. If this book has an advocacy aim, it is perhaps to claim that rights-based discourses can be flexible enough to incorporate the kinds of objectives defined by Puntos. The work can be said to fit with the authors' definition of rights-based work, through its focus on empowerment, attitudinal changes and support for community-based organizational initiatives.

In this context, and despite the rejection of the 'rights-based' label, Puntos' institutional practice is worth highlighting as a good example of well developed (although by no means complete) mechanisms for internal democracy, something central to consistently applied rights-based work. Such structures are by no means a prerequisite for rights-based focuses, but we would contend that they are implied by the philosophy. While many interviewees talked about the importance of consistency between their own discourse and practice as NGOs, their organizations did not always fully reflect this. Puntos was an NGO that was attempting to address this issue in concrete and interesting ways.

Case study 1: Maseualsiuamej Mosenyolchikuanij

Maseualsiuamej Mosenyolchikuanij (MM) is an organization of women from six Nahua communities in the rural region surrounding Cuetzalan, in the Sierra Norte of Puebla, about six hours by bus from Mexico City. It runs a central office and a hotel in the town itself, but is essentially a GRO that operates within a rural context. As such, it provides a useful contrast to the urban-based NGOs that form the main part of this study. A discussion of MM's case ties together a number of threads associated with the proposed shifts from needs/charity/welfare to rights/empowerment. First, MM is a membership organization, and its practices of participatory organization and internal democracy are worth highlighting. Second, the history of MM has been experienced by some of its members as 'progressive empowerment', individually, institutionally and collectively as women. MM began as a small women's section within a male agricultural cooperative, and became a large GRO that supervises development programmes in six communities, as well as running its own hotel. On a more individual level, a number of members told stories highlighting their personal experiences of empowerment through participation in the group, expressing the interaction of the development of 'power from within', 'power with' and 'power to' highlighted by Rowlands (1998). Of course, we also found a notable diversity of experiences and expectations among the members, demonstrating the incompleteness and complexities of the shifts we explore here.

Finally, the case study illustrates a specific example of a more general shift in NGO structure in Latin America, described in the introduction. NGOs that conceived of their role as solely to support community-based groups were qualitatively different from more charitable organizations that combined this kind of work with direct service delivery. That difference is the organizational expression of the shifts in discourse from charity/welfare/needs to rights/empowerment approaches, albeit with attendant contestations and complexities. This case study investigates the relationship between an indigenous GRO and non-indigenous or *mestiza*[33] women, who provided much of the impetus for its founding and thereafter continued to offer technical support, but as a separate institution. The *mestiza* facilitators moved from being effectively the leaders of MM, through what they characterized as a 'divorce', to setting up their own NGO, in order to provide technical and legal support for GROs in the region generally.

The research for this case study was conducted while staying in the hotel run by MM, thus providing some understanding of the reasons behind the success of the hotel, its running and location. Interviews were conducted with three members of the council in the central offices and craft shop of MM, the manager of the hotel (who has a long history of involvement at leadership level with MM) and two of the three facilitators in their office at CADEM. Two communities were visited in the company of another member of the council. One of the authors also attended a general committee meeting and subsequently conducted a participatory group research exercise on the women's understandings of their rights and feelings about the organization.

Context and history

The majority of indigenous people in the Cuetzalan region are farmers. Before the 1970s most were subsistence farmers, but in the period up until 1988, the Mexican government encouraged the monocultivation of coffee for export. The consequent dependence of the region's economy on the international coffee market made it vulnerable to the effects of falls in coffee prices which, combined with the withdrawal of state programmes in support of coffee production, led to growing poverty. This increased migration to the cities of Puebla and Mexico City, leading to the feminization of agricultural labour and consequent prolongation of women's working days, with attendant rise in health problems. In addition, the degradation of the land as a result of monocultivation has made it hard for people to return to subsistence farming, even if they had the labour available to do so.

Furthermore, indigenous women in the region face special difficulties due to their class, ethnic and gender positioning. Those who collaborated with this research spoke of poverty as their principal problem, and mentioned domestic violence, drug addiction, discrimination, lack of resources for education, malnutrition, pollution, an overly long working day, and poorly paid and infrequent jobs. They also identified problems provoked by the migration of the young, particularly those who deny and wish to lose their ethnic identity.

Maseualsiuamej Mosenyolchikauanij means 'Indigenous women who work together and help each other', and the organization constituted itself as a legal entity in 1992. Before then, it was a commission of women artisans within the mixed Regional Agricultural and Livestock Cooperative, 'Tosepan Titatanisque' (Cooperativa Agropecuaria Regional 'Tosepan Titatanisque' or CARTT), with the central objective of selling their craft work (principally weaving and embroidery). The women's commission started in 1985, partly on the initiative of some university students who were carrying out their statutory period of social service there. It started with 50 partners/members (*socias*) from two indigenous rural communities, and by 1989 had expanded to seven communities and 300 members. In 1990, it separated from the cooperative, largely as a result of conflicts generated by its growing size and initiatives to gain external financing of its own. At the time of research, it consisted of 200 members in six communities.

The selling of craftwork continues to form the backbone of the organization's activities. It has a small shop in the town of Cuetzalan, which is also its central office. There, the members sell products such as embroidered blouses, shirts, shawls, scarves, tablecloths and napkins. They also distribute a mail order catalogue throughout Mexico, and have a website advertising their products and activities.[34] Over the years, MM has expanded its activities. In early 1999, it organized them into five project areas linked under three programme headings, with an education and capacity-building programme feeding into all of them. Their activities were as follows:

- economic projects: small enterprises (mills and tortilla making); craft work
- food production and basic health projects: farms (primarily of pigs, fattening and breeding), provision of house-building materials, small gardens, compost, latrine-building, traditional medicine
- ecotourism (a hotel, see Box 16).

Initiatives included workshops on health, particularly the recovery of traditional medicine, but also on women's health from a gender perspective; workshops on human rights, new craft designs, new methods, commercialization of goods, administration and organization.

Box 16   Project evolution and sustainability

The most recent project run by MM is a hotel. Funded through loans from various institutions, led by the World Food Programme, as well as national development and tourist funds, the Hotel Taselotzin (which means 'fruit of the earth' in Nahua) opened on 27 September 1997. The project had been proposed to the general assembly of the partners/members in January 1996. It received funding in April of that year, and construction began in July. The external funding was not sufficient, so 47 shareholders each provided 200 pesos in cash and 10 *faenas* (i.e. units of labour), also worth 200 pesos. The shareholders began to meet regularly, and voted in the supervisory commissions set up to oversee the development of the project. In January 1999, the shareholders decided to meet every three months rather than every month, as previously.

Initially, profits went to the payment of debts and the completion of buildings. The next priority was to pay off the shareholders. According to the facilitators, the ultimate aim for the hotel earnings is to support the organization itself, since despite ample external funds for welfare, nutrition and health projects, there are limited funds available for administration and institutional development. However, it remains to be seen what balance is obtained, once the debts are paid off, between the shareholders' return on their investment and the money that goes to the organization as a whole.

The hotel, which is a good-quality, middle-range establishment, is situated on the hill above Cuetzalan. It was designed with ecological criteria in mind, incorporating, for example, rainwater collection and composting systems. It has two dormitory-style rooms and ten double rooms in single-storey cabins. The rooms are sparsely furnished but elegant and scrupulously clean. The large dining room is the centre-piece of the hotel complex, and members of MM staff the kitchens, cooking regional specialities. During the first years of the project, weekdays were quiet, but Cuetzalan is a highly popular tourist destination for residents of the nearby city of Puebla. MM has made agreements with various tour agencies there, and the hotel is usually full at weekends. It also hosts seminars and meetings, and was beginning to attract more foreign tourists, especially through international ecotourism networks. MM has ambitions for the hotel to become a fully-fledged ecotourism project with education facilities, tour guides and 'traditional indigenous gardens' growing local medicinal plants. It also hopes to expand into the production and marketing of ornamental house plants, recycled paper, traditional medicines and biodegradable cleaning products.

More recently, MM has begun to produce traditional medicines for commercial purposes, opening a pharmacy in Cuetzalan in addition to the craftwork shop.

The organization is oriented towards poverty alleviation, as illustrated by the focus of two of the three programme areas on income generation, as well as comments made by members we interviewed. The third programme area (food production) also comprises needs-oriented projects, incorporating production of food for family consumption, provision of building materials to improve homes and health promotion projects. Yet there are three main aspects of MM which provide indications of the intertwining of needs and rights approaches in practice. These are the extent of internal democracy in the organization, the experience of 'progressive empowerment' in terms of organizational development and for individual women, and finally, the relationship between the GRO and its facilitators.

Internal structure

The highest authority in MM is the yearly general assembly, which all 200 members should attend. Decisions are taken by majority vote, over issues such as evaluations of projects and proposals for new projects. Each community has a local committee, which meets every month to discuss its own projects and plans, and to disseminate information from its council representative. The council is formed by a representative from each local committee, and also meets monthly. As well as the community representation, each council member is in charge of one area of project work, and there are two members present from the previous council to help and train the new council members. In addition, the council can convene 'meetings of committees' as a means of taking decisions that are inappropriate for or cannot wait until the annual assembly. These meetings consist of as many members as can come on the day.

One of the authors attended a general committee meeting of MM, which had three objectives. First, informing the members about, and second, approving, a change in project organization that had been proposed by the council. The third main objective of the meeting was to set dates for general committee meetings for the newly delineated programme areas. By the end of the meeting, which lasted three and a half hours, there were about 25 women present, as well as one of the facilitators. Those present varied in age from their thirties upwards. The first phase of the meeting was bilingual Nahuatl–Spanish, as Estela, the facilitator, did not speak Nahuatl. She waited while important discussions took place and were translated by one of the leaders present. The meeting was led at first by Estela, who began by pointing out the necessity for members to attend these meetings and later to disseminate the information in their own communities. She followed by asking what had been discussed in the general assembly in January. No one was forthcoming, many saying that they couldn't remember. She then went over what they had discussed. One of the main things had been the nomination of a new council, and she explained that this meeting was to approve (or not) what the new council had decided to do. She explained the new structure, using a sheet of paper to systematize the discussions, but not giving a lecture. She then asked what people thought about it, and a couple of women spoke up in agreement. Explanation and discussion in Nahuatl followed, and the consensus decision appeared to be in agreement.

In this first stage, Estela steered the discussion, along with one of the council members and long-standing leaders of MM, Doña Paulina. She also wrote up the conclusions and conducted much of the meeting in Spanish, which may not have been entirely appropriate. While the explanation was going on in Spanish, a number of women were falling asleep and many looked bored. However, Estela did not lecture and allowed for discussion in Nahuatl to take place, ensuring that all present understood the point of the meeting. She also stressed that her presence was on the invitation of the council. In this bilingual phase, the ones who spoke most were not the members of the council, but older women with more confidence. Doña Paulina was most involved, in explaining, commenting and translating between Nahuatl and Spanish, but did not dominate when others wanted to speak, being careful to wait for others to speak even if she knew the answer.

The meeting became more animated in Nahuatl, particularly when discussing the author present and how far she had come. After a refreshment break, the facilitator left and the remaining members continued their discussions in Nahuatl, setting up dates for various committee meetings, discussing prices for craftwork and examining the researcher's project. In the Nahuatl section, relations seemed egalitarian, the discussion was animated and everyone was involved, although the same women as earlier were still doing the most speaking, and Doña Paulina moved the discussion on. This part seemed to be where the majority of the real business of the meeting took place, even though (or perhaps because) it took a long time to decide anything.

There are several conclusions, then, about the participatory and democratic nature of this organization that arise from the above discussion of the general committee meeting.

- Despite the leading role of the facilitator, ownership of decision making was squarely in the hands of the women present. The language barrier may help in this, meaning that discussions can be kept private and consensus reached without the facilitator being involved. However, it may also be a block to communication between the members and the facilitator.

- In the Nahuatl section particularly, relations seemed egalitarian and all were involved in discussion. Of course, this is only an impression, and would need testing through ethnographic research by researchers competent in local, particularly indigenous, languages.
- Despite this egalitarianism, leadership was important. Both sections were effectively led through an alliance of the facilitator and Doña Paulina, the latter being particularly charismatic and well respected.
- The members had an understanding of the need for organizational structure, but were not particularly interested in the details. However, they were very committed to the general discussions and to the progress of the organization.
- Decisions were taken through consensus rather than representative voting. Further investigation of the mechanisms of decision making through consensus would be illuminating, particularly the roles of gender, age and ethnicity in these processes. This is also something that Puntos de Encuentro has discussed.
- The whole event gave the impression of an organization in which the values of cooperation and trust were important indicators of success.

Progressive empowerment?

There are many important ways in which MM exemplifies the process of 'progressive empowerment', as well as illustrating how a shift in focus from needs to rights has occurred. However, this is not to say that such a shift has been experienced in the same way, if at all, by all the women who participate in the organization. There was a marked diversity in the expectations and experiences of the members. Visits to communities, as well as the participatory research exercise, drew out the perception of many members that the most important aspect of MM's existence is to market their craftwork and to address their needs.

Nevertheless, when asked which workshops had been the most interesting, members in the communities visited pointed to those on health and human rights as having been of particular interest to them. Many said that the human rights workshops had helped them to 'defend themselves', to assert their right to control their own work and to be able to leave the house when they wished. This latter was significant because many women had encountered their husbands' resistance to their involvement in the project. Furthermore, comments made during interviews and in the participatory research exercise revealed the ways in which the organization changed their lives for the better, explained in terms that revealed a sense of empowerment.[35]

During discussions after the general committee meeting mentioned earlier, the women present attributed their knowledge of their rights primarily to their membership of the organization. When asked what they considered was the most important result of their participation in the project, they said that it was their 'greater freedom'. Doña Lucia, a woman in her late forties, explained:

Today, it's different from our parents' generation. Now we know that women have the same rights as men. Before, the men decided everything, but we know we have the right to work and to decide for ourselves. At first, our husbands, and sometimes elder sons, didn't want us to be part of the organization. Now we are free to make decisions.

One woman said, to general agreement, that other organizations of women artisans had not 'got there yet', in the sense that their husbands continued to control them:

Their husbands are like ours before, when they controlled what we sold and for how much. Now we make those decisions. Others still have those problems. We don't because we know our rights.

Another said that husbands used to beat their wives, but since they have been part of the organization this no longer happens. She also said that the organization changed their way of thinking with regard to *mestizos* and the authorities: 'Before, if a white or *mestizo* person was nice to us, we felt grateful, and were surprised.' Now they demand to be treated with respect, particularly by the authorities.

Many said that they had learned many things from the organization. This was very important for Doña Alicia, who was only educated to fourth grade. In 1992, she didn't speak Spanish, yet seven years later she was the manager of the hotel and its seven staff. She also regularly travelled around Mexico to promote the hotel, and felt that she was much less timid than before:

I think that my personal manner has changed. Before I was afraid to go out ... now I'm not afraid. I'm even going to go to

Acapulco alone. It's *our* power, because it's *our* decision to go alone, we don't have to wait for another person – we decide and we go. Before, my family said that I couldn't get home late, but when I was in charge of crafts, I sold from 9am to 7pm (and my community is two hours walking from the town). . . . I thank the organization for all that.

Overcoming fear of travelling was seen as vitally important for several of the members of the organization who have left the area, or the country, to market their craftwork and attend meetings. One member had travelled to Quito, Ecuador, and one was due to travel to Canada for a conference on intellectual property rights in craftwork designs. This echoes the findings of other researchers who found similar evidence of empowerment in the contrast painted between a 'before', when the women felt controlled, and an 'after', where they feel a greater power to 'do' things (*'poder "para hacer"'* (Perez Nasser, 1999), and therefore greater autonomy (Townsend et al., 1999; Eccher and Hornes, 2002).

However, evidence of a shift (even if still under way) from needs/welfare to rights/empowerment within MM was not only to be found in informants' subjective assessments. MM's activities had, over the years, broadened from needs-based work around income generation towards more strategic issues of self-subsistence, recovery of culture, women's health and human rights. Notable is the development of the hotel, an ambitious project which was designed specifically to provide a sustainable source of income for the organization. Doña Alicia and Doña Paulina both said that MM had to struggle for its right to undertake such a venture in the face of openly racist and sexist objections from the authorities and the *mestizo* city dwellers, as well as from other hotel owners in Cuetzalan. Eccher and Hornes report that the neighbours 'began to complain, to block the road, threw stones, saying "these women are mad, they won't be able to succeed, they don't have any experience in this"'; and the authorities were similarly dismissive, 'asking "what are these women thinking?"'. Someone even called in the police (Eccher and Hornes, 2002).

Their success in this struggle had contributed to a personal sense of empowerment. Furthermore, members' increased involvement in regional, national and international networks and meetings also provides evidence of a shift towards strategic rights agendas. In addition, Doña Paulina stood for the municipal presidency in a personal capacity, which was a source of pride for many members. This provides more indications of empowerment, if empowerment involves acting to bring about political and policy change as well as the more subjective and personal shifts in behaviour and self-esteem.

However, Doña Paulina's fate also demonstrates the influence of a particular sociopolitical context in the development of rights-based strategies. She was unsuccessful, in no small part because she stood for the Partido Revolucionario Democrático (PRD, Democratic Revolutionary Party), a left-wing party that struggled nationally against the domination of the Partido Revolucionario Institucional (PRI, Institutional Revolutionary Party) in Mexico. As one informant pointed out, the PRI historically 'had more people' (in terms of both active supporters and voters), it 'gave presents' and it therefore usually won the local elections. However, MM was training its members politically, stressing the fact that the vote is a personal decision and secret. This aspect was also pointed to by one informant as an important reason for MM not becoming directly involved in politics, i.e. not dictating for whom members should vote. The strength of the party political system also occasionally provided a barrier to the organization involving itself politically, even independently. Some members supported the PRI, some the PRD (to the left of the PRI) and some the Partido de Acción Nacional (PAN, Party of National Action, to the right of the PRI). This particular informant felt that political involvement would thus provoke more disputes than it is worth. She said she did not think the women were particularly interested in politics: they did not think that things would ever be different, as at the time of our research they thought that the PRI would always win. In fact, the PAN's Vicente Fox won the presidential elections of 2000, a victory that may alter the women's attitudes towards political involvement.

MM's *mestiza* facilitators agreed with the members that there had been a shift in its focus from needs towards rights and empowerment. They maintained that it was a natural progression, and argued that the very fact of women leaving home to travel to Mexico City and sell craft items necessitated some awareness of their rights. They characterized the changes as difficult to achieve, slow and as yet incomplete, but felt that their theoretical input had been vital to any shifts that had occurred. From the beginning, they had striven to incorporate a strong gender focus into all of their activities and the work of MM, a focus which they viewed as a natural outcome of their role. As one summarized it:

For me, you can't be involved in development work without the personal lives of each of those involved being important to you. Some institutions function in this way, only concerning themselves with the work done; and as a result, either the projects fail or only the leaders prosper.

Relationship with facilitators

From the organization's beginning, non-indigenous activists were integral to its development, both structural and conceptual. In fact, one of
the students who encouraged the women of the CARTT to form their
own commission returned a few years later to become an internal full-
time facilitator. The organization had three facilitators, each responsible for one part of the local region. They helped produce materials,
develop funding proposals and project designs, and strengthen the
organizational structure. However, in 1995, the facilitators began
the process of splitting institutionally from MM, leaving it a wholly
indigenous organization, and setting up their own NGO called Centro
de Asesoría y Desarrollo entre Mujeres (the Centre for Advice and
Development with Women, or CADEM). They continue to have
a strong personal investment in MM, and help with funding proposals,
running meetings and providing workshops, etc., but they also provide
advice and educational services for other organizations in the region.

The facilitators had a strong participatory ethos. For example, during
the meeting described above, Estela warmed the members up for later
discussion and retired without fanfare when the coffee came round and
her part was finished, leaving later, again discreetly. The facilitators
also ran the workshops on human rights mentioned above. They held
discussions and then later produced leaflets for distribution that
summarized those discussions, in order to systematize the women's
conclusions and provide participants with a summary of the workshop.
This is in contrast to the majority of organizations we spoke with, who
produced their materials prior to holding the workshop.[36]

The three facilitators considered the separation from MM to have
been an emotionally fraught affair, akin to a divorce. They explained
that it was a natural progression: as the hotel project was being
discussed and the organization was growing, they realized that they
were becoming less indispensable and their views were not being
taken into account. Their participatory focus meant they had not
planned to remain internal facilitators forever, and they were always
keenly aware of their position as *mestiza* women in an indigenous
organization. Furthermore, other groups of women were approaching
them for advice and technical support. Thus, they proposed a separation on the basis of promoting autonomy, as much for themselves as for
MM. From MM's point of view, Doña Paulina explained it thus:

They were helping us full time, but we always took the decisions.
It wasn't our idea, it was theirs [to separate]: for us, it would have

been better if they had continued to be with us, but they decided that they wanted to help other groups of women. And we realized that if we want to grow, we have to learn how to go it alone. If we need them, we call them; but mostly we coordinate in order to do events, forums, etc. Sometimes they come for a little while to our council meetings to give some information, or a chat: a little while, and then they go!

CADEM and MM exemplify an egalitarian relationship between target group and development workers: the operation of participatory development principles in practice. The negotiation of their relationship illustrates the kind of reconfiguration we would contend result from a rights-based focus in development.

Rights in real life

MM's work also illustrates a further point that arose time and again when we were writing this book, that is, the innovative ways in which Latin American NGOs and GROs make human rights relevant to people's day-to-day lives. The members had a very sophisticated awareness of their own gender needs/issues, and an equally sophisticated, practical and non-abstract notion of rights. The details of international human rights legislation were less important to them than their personal understandings of their particular rights. During the group participatory research exercise, the principal kinds of rights they considered they had, and that were important to help address their needs, were described as follows:

- the right to organize, expressed as: 'the right to organize ourselves, to participate, to have and express an opinion, to make decisions; the right to resolve our individual and collective needs'
- the right to earn and manage their own money
- the right to develop a project and gain financing for it
- rights to education and education for their children
- rights to health, and good service at clinics and hospitals
- the right to be taken into account as women, and as indigenous peoples, by the authorities
- the right to demand good payment for their work
- the right to respect and dignity.

This provides some sort of answer to the criticisms of rights-based discourses as overly abstract and irrelevant to ordinary people. Rights function as a vehicle both for presenting strategic demands and, perhaps more importantly, for thinking strategically. The women of MM linked needs to rights not by thinking of their needs and then translating them to rights according to national or international legislation. Instead, they were thinking through ways of addressing their needs and formulating whatever demands had to be made. In this way, rights were understood as a more positive discourse than needs, and also as a way to encourage mobilization. Traditional needs-based focuses can, in contrast, often lead to resignation and passive acceptance of whatever the government or international community is prepared to give as a favour, rather than concede as entitlement.

Case study 2: Puntos de Encuentro, Nicaragua

The Fundación Puntos de Encuentro para Transformar la Vida Cotidiana (Meeting Points for the Transformation of Daily Life Foundation) was set up on the initiative of a small group of feminist activists in 1989, to provide coordination between the different elements of the women's movement in Nicaragua. The fall of the revolutionary Sandinistas in the elections of 1990 sharpened their resolve, as they feared that state support for civil society in general and for the women's movement in particular would disappear. The Sandinistas had provided considerable backing for the women's movement through the party organization AMNLAE (The Luisa Amanda Espinosa Association of Nicaraguan Women). Concentrating on women and young people, Puntos de Encuentro's mission statement claims their goal as 'social change', by which they mean the promotion of equitable relations between men, women, children, young people and adolescents, in both the private and public arenas. They seek to contribute to the empowerment of women and young people, and to the development of their physical, economic, cultural and political autonomy. Puntos operates largely in the urban context of Managua, the capital of Nicaragua, although it also distributes its magazine, *La Boletina*, through a rural network.

The Sandinista Revolution of 1979–90 impacted on both the level of organization among poor Nicaraguans and their expectations of the state. Through FSLN support for the labour and women's movements and through its health and education programmes, large numbers of people received training and gained experience that was transferred after 1990 to the NGO sector. Many people who came from abroad in the early 1980s (*internacionalistas*), drawn by the idealism of the revolution, chose to remain. Some of these have an important role in the NGO field. The director of Puntos de Encuentro, Ana Criquillon, born in France, is a case in point. The Sandinista period also provided some impetus to the women's movement as it became disillusioned with the failure of the revolution to live up to its promises with regard to gender equality (Molyneux, 2000b; González and Kampwirth, 2001). Furthermore, the economic hardship, the war against the US-sponsored Contras and the economic policies of the Sandinista government combined to create a difficult and highly politicized situation. While Nicaragua's economy made some recovery according to formal indicators in the 1990s, it remains heavily dependent on aid.

Puntos de Encuentro is situated in a residential district of Managua. It occupies a sizeable compound and a network of purpose-built offices, teaching and conference rooms, all connected to each other by pleasant walkways and gardens. A café also provides a meeting place for the 30 or so staff and numerous visitors who pass through each day to discuss projects and network. Puntos was at the time of the research a well funded and highly institutionalized organization, with plenty of available space for interviews and discussions. In addition, the existence of an institutional development department helped with the gathering of information. It provided the facilities we needed to conduct our research and made internal evaluation documents and copies of relevant external evaluations freely available to us, in part because we had good prior contacts with Puntos. Yet there was also an evident openness and eagerness to learn from us and share ideas, which formed part of the institutional philosophy. It was the only organization to request feedback from us during the field-work period. As a result we felt that the time with Puntos was mutually beneficial, provoking discussion throughout the organization and raising themes for further thought. Later, Puntos informed us that their participation in the research for this book had been partly responsible for changing the way they viewed their organization, as they moved to a more explicit rights-based approach (Amy Bank, personal conmmunication).

Both of us attended Puntos' events in the course of a week spent with them. We attended the Programme Coordination meeting held at the beginning of our week there, and convened two meetings with programme teams, which included participatory research exercises. We interviewed individuals representing two organizations that attended courses run by the University of Women, and two young users of the Youth Capacity-building programme. We also attended an Organizational Strengthening course and discussed it with the NGO activists present. In addition, numerous informal discussions contributed to our thinking on rights and development issues.

Working for social change

From its inception, Puntos aimed to provide coordination and training, first for the women's movement in Nicaragua, and later expanding to work with groups of young people and for a time with men's groups. It has two main objectives: to impact on public opinion and to strengthen social movements in Nicaragua. It aims to do this primarily through media communication activities and training, supported by research projects for particular campaigns (such as that on masculinities and non-violence) and information services. The communications department produces a magazine and a daily radio programme, as well as a TV soap opera that was in development at the time of our research. The training is primarily aimed at adult women and young people of both sexes.

Communications

Puntos has achieved some national outreach through its feminist magazine for women, *La Boletina*. With a print run of 22 000, it has the widest circulation of any magazine in Nicaragua. It is distributed throughout the country, via a network of volunteers in women's and youth organizations. The May/June/July 1998 magazine covered issues such as lesbian love, male violence, social justice and equality under the law, and women in the Chiapas region of Mexico. Although Puntos had intended *La Boletina* to be distributed to adult women within organizations, an evaluation conducted in 1996 found that they had a very high percentage of young readers between 13 and 24 years old.

The radio programme is explicitly aimed at young people and is transmitted over the university radio channel on weekday evenings. It has a similar audience profile to *La Boletina*, the average age of female listeners being 18 and of male listeners 19. It incorporates various different formats, including interviews, surveys and discussion forums. The programme aims to cover 'themes from daily life through a feminist and anti-adultist perspective: sexuality, violence, relationships between partners, family relationships, reproductive rights, the youth movement, the environment, popular culture, etc.'.[37]

More recently, Puntos developed a TV programme called *Sexto Sentido*, or Sixth Sense, made by young people for young people, and with a similar focus. Funded by the UNIFEM Trust Fund in Support of Actions to Eliminate Violence Against Women, the show was backed up by the radio programme and advocacy campaigns on emergency contraception and domestic violence. It was remarkably successful, becoming the top-rated TV show in its time slot in Managua, with 70% of the TV viewing audience at that time, and an especially large audience in the 13–17 and 18–24 age categories. They have plans to broadcast *Sexto Sentido* in Mexico and Guatemala.[38]

Training

Puntos also conducts various workshops and capacity-building activities. A 'University for Women' project was aimed largely at adult women in social organizations, such as trades unions, community groups and women's groups. At the time of our research, courses addressed:

- ways to develop a gender equality plan within mixed organizations
- monitoring and evaluation of gender aspects in projects
- conflict management
- non-discriminatory forms of working with young people
- income generation projects.

Many of the workers from other Nicaraguan NGOs interviewed had attended Puntos courses and found them on the whole extremely helpful, maintaining that they had an important 'multiplier' effect within their own institutions.

We attended one two-day workshop run by two Puntos workers on developing policies for decision making within women's organizations. The workshop included discussion groups and plenary sessions, held in the large hall where Puntos holds its meetings. The 15 participants, all involved in women's organizations in Nicaragua, discussed decision making in their organizations. The participants were at first divided into three groups of five, then five groups of three, comprising one member of each group, so that everyone was aware of all of the discussions. They then held a plenary session, with the two Puntos workers who had also participated in the small group discussions helping to systematize the groups' conclusions. A number of the participants said they had not previously thought about the importance of explicitly democratic decision-making processes, and they appreciated the opportunity to discuss such issues and to raise questions such as what to do when there is no consensus, and how to break down the division between leadership and workers. On the second day, they discussed issues associated with mixed-gender groups, as well as specific processes for greater democracy in decision making.

The course participants interviewed were very positive about Puntos' role and methodology, highlighting the opportunity such courses gave them to exchange experiences with fellow practitioners and think about the institutional development of their organizations (all NGOs). Rosalia, a development worker from the southern part of Nicaragua, felt that Puntos had improved greatly since 1993, when she had begun attending courses, with better materials, more demanding course content, more convenient timetabling and a greater diversity of themes. However, she had her doubts about the application of institutional development ideas from the commercial sector being applied to the NGO sector, and she had discussed this with those in charge of the course. She was exemplary of many of the women participating, who saw themselves as Puntos' partners rather than its pupils. Their main criticism was that Puntos did not provide enough follow-up after courses.

At the time of our research Puntos also conducted around four or five capacity-building workshops per year, as well as an annual ten-day camp, with young people (aged 16–25). Those who qualified for capacity building were under 25 and usually had leadership positions in youth groups. The capacity building was aimed at strengthening Nicaraguan youth movements. When asked to assess the most important impacts they hoped for from this programme, the project teams in charge highlighted the following:

- construction of a generational identity as a subject of rights; autonomy
- sensitivity to and respect for diversity based in equality
- construction of equal relations between people: adults and young people, men and women, etc.

Not only did the young people have a chance to reflect on and analyse their daily life, and learn more about issues surrounding gender, generation and sexuality, but the capacity-building enterprises, especially the annual camp, also promoted the development of new networks.

The two young people we interviewed who had participated in the camps were extremely enthusiastic about Puntos, maintaining that it dealt with issues that no other organization in Nicaragua was prepared to treat. Sofia, a 23-year-old who works in another Nicaraguan women's organization, pointed out that other NGOs didn't focus their efforts on young people at all, and she felt that they certainly didn't deal with themes such as racism and 'adultism'. She said 'it's the only organization like it, and it seems good to me'. Both highlighted the importance of Puntos' methodology for them. They felt it to be novel, and appreciated the more personal and introspective aspects in that it made them analyse their own lives, rather than dictating to them, or only concentrating on practical issues. They particularly emphasized the focus on dialogue and sharing. Andres, an 18-year-old, said:

> [Puntos] gave me a new vision of the world, made me look with different eyes at society and at my own self. . . . I would say that Puntos plays a little bit with people's feelings, in a positive way though, to make people reflect on themselves, and to be able to change the patterns in their lives. . . . I think it is very important. The thing is not just to oblige other people to change, but to make us reflect within ourselves, and say, 'OK, I'm wrong here'.

Finally, a short-lived Masculinity project conducted capacity-building workshops, raising awareness of the ways in which masculinity is constructed and some of the reasons for male violence. It also aimed to debate masculinity more generally, through print media, radio and television, and undertook an important research project on male violence.

Guiding philosophy: rights or autonomy?

Puntos preferred to work with the theme of autonomy rather than human rights. They defined autonomy as 'the right and capacity to act and participate in decisions that affect the person or group, without having to subordinate oneself to the "other"'[39] This contrasts with many of the other organizations in this study, which tended to see autonomy as an integral component of human rights and essential to their idea of agency. Puntos staff had an instinctively negative initial reaction to working for the advancement of human rights, partly on account of the context in which they worked. Ana Criquillon explained:

> I think that the way in which people have worked with the theme of human rights in Nicaragua has been an idea that women's rights and human rights are more about the defence of individual rights, and we don't work very much with women's individual rights. Of course, you defend these rights because collectively you have them. But if a woman comes to the office here and says 'You know what? They aren't respecting my personal auton- omy', we would probably say, 'Look, that's how it is, it's the same for all of us. What can we do *collectively* to confront this?' We decided to work collectively so that women's rights can become reality, whereas here [in Nicaragua] the defence of human rights is always treated on a case-by-case basis.

These comments indicate a concern, characteristic of much socialist criticism of human rights, that human rights foster individualism rather than being part of a collective project for social change. Other members of staff saw human rights as a complex issue, and highlighted the need to analyse the way that privileged sectors construct their own human rights through the violation or reduction of the rights of others.

Puntos chose to focus on autonomy as providing an alternative to a focus on the individual subject of rights conceived in more abstract and legalistic terms. While they acknowledged that the idea of autonomy is also based on a notion of the individual, in their conception individuals were conceived of as embodied and embedded in social relations, in contrast to what they saw as classical notions of abstract rights-bearing subjects found in liberal discourse and in the dominant political discourse in Nicaragua. In this respect, Puntos was particularly influenced by Marcela Lagarde's work (Lagarde, 1998, 2000). Ana Criquillon also highlighted the importance of Nicaragua's history in shaping Puntos's views of its own work. She associated human rights with earlier campaigns against the Somoza dictatorship, which focused on the condemnation of state violations of rights, and asserted that Puntos wanted to move from 'denunciation' to develop positive proposals for change. Such a focus had never been part of human rights culture in Nicaragua. She felt that this was partly to do with the revolution:

> The revolution here helped us to make the transition from dictatorship . . . to a point when they said 'OK, now we are in power, now finally, the denunciations have finished, now what? There's been a lot of talk but what do you propose?' Well, of course, there was no easy answer, because even when we [women] were proposing alternatives, they didn't listen to us very much. But it was a challenge to respond to and there was a lesson to be learned. I think that we at Puntos learnt to value the impact that you can have if you come out and propose alternatives.

Criquillon believed that this reflected an evolution in the thinking of the left, from a denunciatory culture during the dictatorship (which was entirely appropriate as all rights were systematically violated) to an attempt to do something constructive during and after the Sandinista period. While some parts of the left either returned to or remained in a mode of confrontation and denunciation, Puntos distanced itself from this stance, seeing it as an abdication of responsibility in a context where widespread deprivation demanded a more constructive response.

As noted earlier, despite their reservations about human rights, Puntos staff identified priorities that overlapped with those identified by other organizations committed to rights-based strategies. In their practice they also shared similar aims: in participatory research exercises for example, they stated that they worked to fulfil the need for greater communication between the sexes and among young people for the construction of a sense of identity as a person, for the creation and strengthening of political and feminist spaces, and access to resources and public policies for young people. They considered freedom from discrimination and 'judgement' (i.e. prejudice) as needs for young people in particular.

When asked if such 'needs' might also be considered as rights, they acknowledged the overlap. Following group discussion during one participatory session, a coherent and full list of the rights they work for was produced. These included rights of association, participation in local and national spaces, freedom of expression (including sexual expression), rights to equality, education, information, respect for difference and physical integrity. In discussion, Puntos staff were not always negative about rights. Some felt that properly conceptualized they might provide more legitimacy for their proposals for change; and that thinking in terms of rights required a questioning of power relations. Furthermore, many were intrigued with the authors' approach to rights-based work as offering something positive and concrete, akin to their conceptualization of empowerment/autonomy. Ana Criquillon also said:

> We always identified ourselves with empowerment, development and autonomy. Of course, they are all rights, but the conceptual entry point was never through rights. However, in some sense, all Puntos' work aims at the obtaining of all women's rights. . . . We should perhaps reclaim the mantle of struggles for women's rights for *positive* work, and not simply equate 'denunciatory' positions with human rights, while we do something else. In fact, we don't do something else, we do the same, just with different strategies.

Puntos is not a typical human rights organization in that it does not involve itself in legal and judicial spheres. This work was felt to be particularly difficult in the context of a government that was promoting a conservative, Catholic agenda, and which was considered corrupt and inefficient. However, Puntos' aims and objectives can be seen in terms of promoting certain rights, in particular rights to autonomy and organization. In addition, its magazine, *La Boletina*, provides information on women's rights for its target audience – women's organizations throughout Nicaragua.

Puntos aims to influence public opinion and public policies, but has found the government to be less than open to its ideas. Other Nicaraguan organizations expressed similar suspicions of the government's political will and its tendency to renege on its promises. It may therefore have been an appropriate choice not to waste too much effort in pressuring the government directly, and to orient Puntos' focus towards the general population, particularly young people. Its work and aims were, however, consistent with a flexible notion of rights-based approaches, even if it did not explicitly identify itself with such an approach.

Internal democracy and organizational structure

As argued in Chapter 7, the participatory nature of rights-based approaches to development implies democratic and egalitarian relationships on a number of different levels. Among the most complex, in terms of implementation, are the relationships between those working for NGOs. Puntos has given much thought to creating structures for effective internal democracy to encourage the full participation of all its workers in the running of the organization. As the example of the workshop described above shows, it was also attempting to share its thinking on this theme with other organizations. Here we discuss Puntos' structure as an example of good practice.

The organizational structure of Puntos is divided into four administrative departments:

- Communication, responsible among other things for the magazine, radio programme and projected TV programme.
- Training, comprising the University for Women, the Youth Capacity-building Programme and the Masculinity programme.
- Investigation and documentation, comprising the campaign research department and information services.
- Administration and finance, which includes a small department responsible for institutional development.

Coordination and decision making occur through three main bodies that meet once a month, and during which decisions are taken by consensus. These are:

- the *Coordinación Programatica* (Programme Coordination), which brings together *all* the people working in the programme teams and administration
- the *Coordinación Atencion a Usuari@s*[40] (Service to Users Coordination), attended by all those, including administrative

personnel, who work in service delivery internally and externally, such as the café and library
- the *Coordinación Administrativa* (Administrative Coordination), bringing together heads of programmes and departments throughout the institution.

The whole institution is characterized by a desire to encourage horizontal participation of all its staff. Even the architectural plan of the building is designed to encourage interacting flows between offices, through the attractive central garden area with its café on-site. One of the sessions of the *Coordinación Programatica* that we attended encouraged group discussions and free expression of opinion on topics such as how Puntos should decide on attending outside events, for example those run by donor agencies, and also the possibility of changing institutional objectives and plans for the following year. The session began with what they called a '*coescuchar*' ('co-listening'), where staff were encouraged to talk for five minutes with someone in the organization whom they didn't know well. The atmosphere was very congenial, if slightly chaotic. Making decisions was a lengthy process, one of the obvious risks associated with the ambitious aim of making decisions collectively and through consensus in a group of over 50 people. Several individuals did dominate the general discussions, even though they did not prevent others from speaking. Furthermore, the meeting had a tendency to create additional administrative work, for example by nominating groups of people to design a participatory process in order to then create a code of conduct for the office. However, it was an opportunity to create institutional cohesion and to share ownership of the running of the organization. It was also an opportunity to explain this particular research project and set up meetings with members of the different programme teams.

Differences in age, experience, commitment, position and knowledge meant that there was an informal hierarchy operating within Puntos. The exchange of information relied mainly on the internal e-mail network and not such collective instances as that described above. Those with well thought-out arguments were in a good position to influence the consensus; also those with greater self-confidence. However, the *formal* mechanisms were horizontal and egalitarian, and the use of small group discussions within the meeting did allow everyone to have their say, even if they did not then contribute to the general discussion.

Moreover, Puntos did not confine its democratic commitment to such meetings. In the late 1990s, it established an affirmative hiring policy in favour of young people (25 and under). As a result, some programmes, particularly those directed at young people, were staffed by young people themselves, and this had an impact on the way the organization worked. For example, the theme of 'adultism' had come much more to the fore, and the 'adults' within Puntos had had to question their own attitudes. In addition, the young people pushed more new issues up the agenda, such as ethnicity, class and disability.

At the time of research, Puntos did not involve users in its strategic meetings, even in the *Coordinación Atención a Usuari@s*. It was considering exploring this in the future, according to the Institutional Development department. Ana Criquillon felt that NGOs often underestimated their users, fearing that they might think in a short-termist manner; but she argued that there was always negotiation in any process of planning, and people needed to understand that no one owns Puntos, neither users nor staff. Clearly also there would be practical issues to resolve, such as the possibility of holding meetings with users during office hours. Yet the fact that internally democratic mechanisms were in place with regard to staff should facilitate effective participation of users in the future.

The example of Puntos shows that an *explicit* rights focus is not a necessary condition for a concerted attempt at institutional democracy or other aspects of rights-based approaches. Other more explicitly rights-based organizations that also work for autonomy, equality, justice and democracy do not have such thorough formal mechanisms for encouraging internal democracy as are evident in Puntos. The theme that was most often brought up by those in Puntos was the importance of consistency. As Ana Criquillon said:

> I think that since Puntos began, those of us who founded Puntos have been very concerned with consistency, between practice and discourse. . . . If you have an institution that doesn't practise what it is proposing in terms of its values, of equity, etc., you'll have a superficial discourse. . . . If it doesn't come from the guts and the heart, it doesn't have any impact.

Other organizations may strive for this in theory but have done less to incorporate the measures necessary to build it into their practice. The extent of internal democracy found in Puntos is in large measure due to the institutional vision of its founders on the one hand and, as is clear from Criquillon's remarks above, from the philosophy that the organization as a whole has maintained since its foundation. Further helpful factors may be the organization's relative youth and the notable willingness by some key donors to allow their funds to be used for institutional development.

Conclusions

As we hope to have shown, the recent emphasis on integrating ideas derived from broader democratic principles into development work has presented NGOs with new challenges and opportunities. A consequence of the human rights movement's advocacy in the international arena and subsequent legislative developments, it has opened up new areas for work within the development field. It has also reframed priorities, objectives and styles of working. In illustrating some of the ways in which 'rights-based approaches to development' have been translated into NGO practice within the Latin American context, we have identified the elements that distinguish it from earlier approaches. These include the promotion of principles of institutional democracy and accountability, a commitment to practices which aim to secure meaningful forms of participation and empowerment, and the integration of rights into development praxis. While these ideas are not in themselves new, in their combination they acquired a special significance during a favourable international context. However limited and politically contingent their continued adoption might eventually prove to be, they have met with considerable enthusiasm in regions undergoing democratic reform.

The Latin American region is notable for the innovative way in which rights have been absorbed into the language and practice of NGOs. The development practitioners we discuss here work with human rights in a variety of ways and arenas, from the local to the national and international. They seek to integrate rights into national development projects, while initiating local projects which promote awareness and activism related to specific rights campaigns. They also engage in legal reform at national and international levels through lobbying and advocacy. Rights are conceived of as indivisible, as including civil, political, social and economic rights, and are pursued as a means to create a more democratic and socially just society. Latin American NGOs have not only developed practical ways of working with rights, but they have sought to combine the pursuit of formal rights with practices that aim to make existing rights more meaningful or substantive. They have also worked to expand the scope of rights-based demands to more fully encompass practical needs while at the same time reframing these needs in more strategic terms.

A central component of this work is the linking of rights to subjective and personal transformation. This process reframes the concept of empowerment by connecting it to ideas of a common humanity, dignity and independent agency. Empowerment is understood as the enhancement of self-esteem combined with a capacity to *act on the world* – to promote structural changes that benefit both individuals and collectivities as well as society as a whole. In post-authoritarian Latin America, these ideas and practices are often expressed in the idiom of citizenship and democracy, understood as a society-wide project of social and political transformation. Empowerment is therefore seen as multidimensional, involving a subjective shift towards greater agency and, when associated with ideas of rights and entitlement, it implies strategizing for political and social change.

For NGOs who work with low-income and disempowered groups such as those discussed here, rights-based approaches are a means to strengthen the claims of these groups to resources of different kinds: economic, political, judicial and social. Through strategies that place the individual subject of rights at the centre of development, they seek to enhance marginalized people's sense of themselves as agents of change. No longer treated as the objects of policies and the target of interventions designed to meet objectives defined by outside agencies, such groups become active subjects, engaged in defining their own needs and aware of their rights and entitlements. In these ways, human rights find an application within the grass roots. When assumed on a personal level they can promote changes in social relations (among family members, between employers and employees) and enhance self-esteem as individuals seek to achieve some greater degree of recognition and self-realization. An essential element of rights work from this perspective is to treat it as a collective endeavour, with group action and identification acting to enhance the capacity of disempowered groups to tackle the structural inequalities which limit their potential for participation in the wider society, whether as economic agents or citizens. This perspective clearly differs from that which dismisses rights-based work as abstracted from the lives and concerns of ordinary people.

Such approaches to rights-based development clearly imply a redefinition of the relationship between development practitioners and the communities they work with, reflected in the language shift from 'beneficiaries' or 'clients' of the NGOs, to 'users'. This has accompanied an endorsement of bottom-up and 'people-centred' development involving the participation of those most in need, and recognized as an essential counterpart to government and agency intervention. Successfully managed NGOs are actively engaged in developing ways of making their commitment to participation more thoroughgoing, mostly through internal consultative mechanisms. When combined with ideas of rights and human dignity, proper treatment, tolerance and respect for difference, this work can play a vital role in transforming political and civil culture, itself a prerequisite for sound democracy and meaningful citizenship.

Participatory and rights-based philosophies of development practice have other implications for NGOs as institutions beyond attempts to reorganize their practice in more democratic ways. NGOs welcome the changes in NGO–donor relations that the commitment to *partnership* implies, so long as it is genuine and treats them as more than agencies merely implementing donors' policies. They feel that donors should recognize the importance of qualitative evaluation mechanisms for rights work, value the considerable NGO expertise in this area and respond to their need for further technical assistance. For partnerships to work, they must be premised on the acknowledgement that NGOs need funds for administrative work and institution building, not just for project delivery. They also hope that donor agencies will see their way to funding more rights-based activities, with medium- and long-term aims.

Translating rights to local settings

Despite broadly positive soundings from NGOs, rights-based development has its sceptics and its opponents, even in Latin America, where the experience of transition from authoritarian rule gives issues of rights and democracy a special significance. Ideas of rights, good governance and participation have not always been enthusiastically accepted by governments, and even where they acquire government support, a wide gulf remains between recognition in theory and support in practice. Different understandings of rights agendas and disagreements over priorities are bound to divide governments from NGOs, and there will be considerable variation in approach across countries and regions depending on the political conditions that prevail. Context matters more than usually for the success or failure of this approach. Where interventions to promote rights have been successful, it is because they have responded to the priorities expressed by locally based democratic social movements, communities and disadvantaged groups themselves. While democratic principles applied to development projects can find application in a broad range of settings, to be effective they have to undergo a degree of adaptation and translation within different regional contexts and cultural and legal systems. Development agencies that are deploying rights-based agendas in Latin America are finding ways of translating macro-level juridical concepts into variable micro-level practices. The gap between rhetorical and/or legal recognition of rights and people's ability to *exercise* those rights is the space where most of the NGOs we researched located their work.

The ways in which development practitioners in Latin America have absorbed rights into their work have therefore provided some insights into how they could achieve a broader international application. While it is necessary to acknowledge the distinctive characteristics of other regions such as Africa or South Asia, and to recognize how they differ as much from each other as from Latin America, NGOs all over the world are dealing with similar issues of poverty, violence and structural inequality, and are working with similar aims and means. Despite the variations in legislative structure, the forms and limits of institutionalized democracy and other sociopolitical variables, there is considerable scope for working on a range of common issues raised by the rights-based agenda. Human rights can be understood as a transversal language with which to represent demands, and a mechanism for thinking strategically. Rights-based strategies have an appeal for many NGOs and GROs not only because they have some support from the broader international development consensus, but because they can be applied and adapted to local circumstances.

If rights are to be integrated into development practice they should be thought of as indivisible and as part of a coherent development strategy. Advocates and development practitioners should guard against narrow definitions of rights as civil and political, and assert that economic, social and cultural rights are central to development. Rights-based development is best seen as an underlying philosophy informing the way that development strategies or projects are conceived. It can succeed only if it is part of a broader development strategy aimed at improving the potential for sustainable development, both human and economic. It is important to stress that for all the positive aspects of rights-based work in the area of poverty elimination and development, the activists we interviewed believed that the success of rights projects, and of the broader aims with which they were associated, depended crucially on governments facing up to and tackling persistent levels of poverty and deprivation. What the inclusion of rights into development signifies, however, is a challenge to technocratic interventions decreed from above and applied with scant regard for those who are most

affected by them. Rights help to address inequalities and power relations in decision making, and as such imply that development must
henceforth be seen as a process of negotiation with all those who are
implicated in it, including those who have so far gained little from it.
These – 'the poor', the subaltern, the disempowered and the disenfran-
chised – are becoming subjects of rights, citizens and participants. As
such they are acquiring enhanced voice and agency, the right to be
heard and the right to act in defence of their own interests. Only time
will tell what effect they will have.

Appendix
NGOs mentioned in this book

Interviewees were speaking in a personal capacity and not as official representatives of their organization.

Names and addresses

Centro de Promoción de la Mujer Gregoria Apaza
Casilla 12571
La Paz, Bolivia
e-mail: gregoria@utama.bolnet.bo

CIDEM, Centro de Información y Desarrollo de la Mujer
Casilla 14036
La Paz, Bolivia
e-mail: cidem@caoba.entelnet.bo

Colectivo Gaviota
Managua, Nicaragua

DEMUS, Estudio para la Defensa de los Derechos de las Mujeres
Caracas 2624
Lima 11, Peru
e-mail: demus@amauta.rcp.net.pe

Flora Tristan, Centro de la Mujer Peruana
Parque Hernan Velarde 42
Lima 1, Peru
e-mail: flora@flora.org.pe
website: www.Flora.org.pe

FOVIDA, Fomento de la Vida
Av. Javier Prado Oeste No. 109
Lima 17, Peru
e-mail: postmast@fovida.org.pe

GIN, Grupo de Initiativa Nacional del Niño y de la Niña
Calle Reni 243
San Borja
Lima, Peru
e-mail: gin@junin.itete.com.pe

ISLI, Instituto de Servicios Legales e Investigacion Juridica
Casilla 12308
La Paz, Bolivia
e-mail: islilpz@entelnet.bo

Manuela Ramos
Av. Juan P Fernandini 1550
Lima 21, Peru

SERPAJ, Servicio Paz y Justicia
Apdo Postal 305
Managua, Nicaragua
e-mail: serpaj@ibw.com.ni

TAHIPAMU
Casilla 2615
La Paz, Bolivia

TAREA
Parque Osores 161
Pueblo Libre, Apartado 2234
Lima 100, Peru
e-mail: postmaster@tarea.org.pe

Case studies

Nicaragua

Fundación Puntos de Encuentro para la Transformación de la Vida
Cotidiana
Apartado Postal RP-39
Managua, Nicaragua
e-mail: puntos@puntos.org.ni
website: www.puntos.org.ni

Mexico:

CADEM
Carranza No. 18
Cuetzalan, Puebla
Mexico
e-mail: cadem@laneta.apc.org

Maseualsiuamej Mosenyolchicauanij
Calle 2 de abril No. 2
73560 Cuetzalan, Puebla
Mexico
e-mail: maseualsiua@laneta.apc.org
website: www.laneta.apc.org/maseualsiua

Hotel Taselotzin
Yoloxochitl S-N
Barrio Tenamicoyan
Cuetzalan, Puebla
Mexico
(information tel: +52 233 10480)

Endnotes

1 Documents consulted include those produced by organizations such as the UK Department for International Development, the Foreign and Commonwealth Office, the Dutch Foreign Office, UNDP, UNICEF, Oxfam, Save the Children UK, International Planned Parenthood Federation and Amnesty International.

2 Paper presented at CEPAL conference, September 2001. See www.eclac.cl

3 The word does not have a Spanish equivalent but women's movement usages range from the neologism *empoderamiento* to *potenciamiento* and *poderio*.

4 For further discussion of these issues, see Townsend et al. (1999).

5 See IDS Topic Pack, Introduction to Participatory Rural Appraisal, for a discussion of Rapid Rural Appraisal methodology.

6 NGOs such as Puntos suffer as well as benefit from changes in donor priorities. Puntos went on to experience leaner years as donors sought to diversify their recipients and programmes.

7 Kirsten Hastrup has pointed out the distinction between the reliance of much of the force of human rights legislation on natural law on a declared general set of rights rather than the specific rights and corresponding duties of positive law (Hastrup, 2001). This declarative, or performative, aspect of rights is underlined by the US Declaration of Independence: 'We hold these Truths to be self-evident, that all Men are created equal, that they are endowed by their Creator with certain unalienable Rights, that among these are Life, Liberty and the Pursuit of Happiness'. (Available at http://memory.loc.gov/const/declar.html)

8 A good example of this, and of some of the power of using rights-based language, is in discussions of the right to health in the USA. As *The Economist* report pointed out, the USA could be accused of violating its citizens' right to health. The writers argue that this is a problem, because the USA will not be brought 'on-side' by such criticisms (*The Economist*, 2001). However, we would argue

that one of the benefits of thinking about such issues in terms of rights is that developed countries are just as open to criticism as developing ones. Still, development agencies tend to be very careful to stress that governments can protect the right to health of their population through privately provided health services, and the usual reason given for this is resource scarcity.

9 Particularly notable were those in Guatemala (1985), Nicaragua (1986), Brazil (1988), Colombia (1991), Mexico (1992), Bolivia (1994) and Venezuela (1999). Panama (1997), Paraguay (1992) and Peru (1993) have made important constitutional statements with regard to indigenous rights (Stavenhagen, 2002).

10 All interviewees' names are pseudonyms.

11 The clear exceptions to this generalization were Cuba and Mexico, which throughout the decade remained one-party states.

12 Authors' interviews.

13 Although the government did not encourage NGO participation, some were able to collaborate with leftist elements within the Catholic Church to ensure their views were fed to the state via the parallel dialogue run by the Church and Jubilee 2000.

14 Interview from 1998.

15 See for example the sections on Puntos de Encuentro in Chapter 8.

16 GIN (Grupo de Initiativa Nacional del Niño y de la Niña) is a children's network in Peru; CIDEM (Centro de Información y Desarrollo de la Mujer) and Gregoria Apaza are both women's organizations in Bolivia; Manuela Ramos is a women's organization in Peru.

17 See www.undp.org/rblac/gender/index.html

18 www.unitem-undp.org

19 www.undp.org/rblac/gender/natcamp.htm

20 www.flora.org.pe

21 www.undp.org/rblac/gender/mens.htm

22 *Cholo* is a term used in the Andes to refer to indigenous people who have moved from the countryside to live in the city. It is usually derogatory.

23 Although in some instances, essentialization of identity is a key strategy, it comes with an implied 'fixity' of culture and identity that might not actually be part of people's lived experience. For example, Jane Cowan discusses the ambiguities of the actions of NGOs that are attempting to represent and at the same time create a Macedonian minority within Northern Greece (Cowan, 2001).

24 For example, DFID's core indicators for measuring progress towards greater gender equality do include education and literacy indicators, but are predominantly about health and reproduction:

child malnutrition rates, infant mortality, maternal mortality, births attended by skilled health personnel, contraceptive prevalence, HIV prevalence (DFID, 2000b: 24).

25 Latin American development practitioners (as well as those in other countries) use 'sustainable' to describe projects which can have an impact in the long term without continuing to rely on the existence of external development funds.

26 They can be summarized by the following categories: attitude change, legislative change, capacity building, the development of personal strategies to deal with individual problems such as violence, and the training of networks of legal, human rights, development or health promoters. The objectives of our case study organizations are described in detail in Chapter 8.

27 See Box 3, describing FOVIDA's definition of politicization in the context of evaluation methods.

28 In Bolivia and Peru, great stress is placed on formal forms of address, such as *usted* (the polite version of the singular 'you'), and *Don* and *Doña*, terms placed at the beginning of people's names, to denote respect. This is important, particularly when addressing elderly people. Indigenous people tend to preserve the polite forms among themselves, where whites or *mestizos* would be more likely to move into addressing each other as '*tu*', the more informal second person form of address. In both Bolivia and Peru, even elderly indigenous people are still often addressed as '*tu*' by young whites, which expresses their subordinate social position and is pejorative and patronizing.

29 Inconsistencies between public proclamations and actual practice are difficult to examine in depth and would need more time to ascertain than was available during the research for this book. The interviews conducted are all situated accounts, presenting the public face of these NGOs for a particular understanding of who makes up the audience.

30 *Adultismo* – a neologism coined by the NGO itself.

31 Since this research was completed Puntos has redefined itself as a rights-based organization.

32 The Latin American Spanish word for this is *asesoras*. It refers to consultants, usually professionals or experienced development workers, who provide NGOs with technical advice and act as knowledge sharers and facilitators of workshops and meetings.

33 *Mestizo/a* is a Latin American ethnic term for people of mixed European and indigenous descent.

34 www.laneta.apc.org/maseualsiua

35 It is important to note that the participatory research exercise was conducted at the end of the general committee meeting mentioned above, and thus included those women committed enough to the organization to attend a central meeting. Some scepticism might be in order here, as this organization has been well researched by feminists eager to find empowerment, and there is the possibility that these women, as well as being the most committed MM members, were also telling the author what they thought she would like to hear.

36 The sources for this assertion are the interview with facilitators and their leaflets. The authors did not attend an actual workshop, but it is instructive that this is the first time this type of structure was explicitly mentioned. However, there are logistical reasons why this was possible, given that they were providing the workshops for one organization with an already existing structure that facilitates distribution *post hoc*.

37 Internal documents, Puntos de Encuentro.

38 UNIFEM press release, 7 August 2002 (www.unifem.undp.org).

39 Internal document, Puntos de Encuentro 1998.

40 Puntos' use of this symbol is explained as follows: 'Many people do not want to use only the masculine when they refer to both men and women. Our language is *machista* and uses the masculine form when referring to both men and women . . . @ represents both men and women' (personal communication).

References

Abel, C. and Lewis, C.M. (Eds) (2002) *Exclusion and Engagement: social policy in Latin America*. London: Institute of Latin American Studies.

Alvarez, S.E. (1998) Latin American feminisms 'go global': trends of the 1990s and challenges for the new millennium, in Alvarez, S.E., Escobar, A. and Dagnino, E. (Eds) *Cultures of Politics, Politics of Cultures. Revisioning Latin American social movements*. Boulder, CO: Westview Press, pp.293–324.

Alvarez, S.E., Escobar, A. and Dagnino, E. (Eds) (1998) *Cultures of Politics, Politics of Cultures. Revisioning Latin American social movements*. Boulder, CO: Westview Press.

Amnesty International (2001) Amnesty International press release 28/08/2001: International Council Meeting: an agenda for human rights in the 21st century, AI index, POL 21/003/2001. London: Amnesty International.

Arosteguí, J., CIET Internacional et al. (1996) Informe de Resultados – Evaluación Global 1991–1996. Managua: Puntos de Encuentro.

Avina, J. (1993) 'The evolutionary life cycles of non-governmental development organizations', *Public Administration and Development* 13(5): 453–474.

Barbalet, J.M. (1988) *Citizenship. Rights, struggle and class inequality*. Milton Keynes: Open University Press.

Bebbington, A. and Thiele, G. (Eds) (1993) *Non-governmental Organizations and the State in Latin America: rethinking roles in sustainable agricultural development*. London: Routledge.

Bejar, H. and Oakley, P. (1995) From accountability to shared responsibility: NGO evaluation in Latin America, in Edwards, M. and Hulme, D. (Eds) *Non-governmental Organisations – Performance and Accountability: beyond the magic bullet*. London: Save the Children and Earthscan, pp.73–82.

Beltrán Sánchez, M. (2001) 'Gregoria Apaza' Women's Center inter-cultural focus and community mobilization to eliminate gender violence. An experience from the El Alto municipality', paper presented at the 2001 symposium 'Gender violence, health and rights in the Americas', Cancun, Mexico, 4–7 June.

Blondet, C. (2002) The 'devil's deal': women's political participation and authoritarianism in Peru, in Molyneux, M. and Razavi, S. (Eds) *Gender Justice, Development and Rights*. Oxford: Oxford University Press.

Bøås, M. (1998) 'Governance as multilateral development bank policy: the cases of the African Development Bank and the Asian Development Bank'. *European Journal of Development Research* 10(2): 117–134.

Bretton Woods (2002) Bretton Woods Update No. 29, July/August.

Bruch, S.A. (Ed.) (1998) *Género y Ciudadanía: una construcción necesaria*. CIDEM-REPEM, La Paz, Bolivia.

Brysk, A. (1994) Acting globally: Indian rights and international politics in Latin America, in Van Cott, D.L. (Ed.) *Indigenous Peoples and Democracy in Latin America*. New York: St Martin's Press, pp.29–51.

Cáceres Valdivia, E., Beltrán Velarde, B. and Caro Velazco, E. (1998) *Mujer, Liderazgo y Desarrollo. Reflexiones de Una Experiencia*. Lima: FOVIDA.

Caulfield, C. (1997) *Masters of Illusion: the World Bank and the poverty of nations*. Oxford: Oxford University Press.

Centro de Promoción de la Mujer Gregoria Apaza (1997) *Diagnóstico Participativo del Distrito 6 de la Ciudad de El Alto*. La Paz: Gregoria Apaza.

Chambers, R. (1997) *Whose Reality Counts? Putting the first last*. London: ITDG Publishing.

Charlesworth, H. and Chinkin, C. (Eds) (2000) *The Boundaries of International Law*. Manchester: Manchester University Press.

Chavez, M.E. (2000) Slave women's strategies for freedom and the late Spanish colonial state, in Dore, E. and Molyneux, M. (Eds) *Hidden Histories of Gender and State in Latin America*. Durham and London: Duke University Press.

CIDEM-REPEM (1996) *Memoria Foro Género y Ciudadanía. La Paz, 18 al 21 de julio de 1996*. La Paz, Bolivia: CIDEM-REPEM.

Cornwall, A. and Gaventa, J. (2000) 'From users and choosers to makers and shapers. Repositioning participation in social policy', *IDS Bulletin* 31(4): 50–62.

Cornwall, A., Lucas, H. and Pasteur, K. (2000) 'Accountability through participation. Developing workable partnership models in the health sector', *IDS Bulletin* 31(1): 1–13.

Corrêa, S. (1997) 'From reproductive health to sexual rights: achievements and future challenges', *Reproductive Health Matters* 10: 107–116.

Cowan, J.K. (2001) Ambiguities of an emancipatory discourse: the making of a Macedonian minority in Greece, in Cowan, J.K., Dembour, M.-B. and Wilson, R. (Eds) *Culture and Rights: anthropological perspectives*. Cambridge: Cambridge University Press.

Cowan, J.K., Dembour, M.-B. and Wilson, R. (Eds) (2001) *Culture and Rights: anthropological perspectives*. Cambridge: Cambridge University Press.

Craske, N. and Molyneux, M. (Eds) (2002) *Gender and the Politics of Rights and Democracy in Latin America*. Houndmills: Palgrave.

Dagnino, E. (1998) Culture, citizenship and democracy: changing discourses and practices of the Latin American left, in Alvarez, S.E., Escobar, A. and Dagnino, E. (Eds) *Cultures of Politics, Politics of Cultures. Revisioning Latin American social movements*. Boulder, CO: Westview Press, pp.33–63.

Dembour, M.-B. (1996) Human rights talk and anthropological ambivalence: the particular context of universal claims, in Harris, O. (Ed.) *Inside and Outside the Law*. London: Routledge.

DFID (1997) *White Paper on International Development*. London: Department for International Development.

DFID (2000a) Making government work for poor people. Building state capability. Strategies for achieving the international development targets. London: Department for International Development.

DFID (2000b) Poverty eradication and the empowerment of women (consultation document). Strategies for achieving the international development targets. London: Department for International Development.

DFID (2000c) Realising human rights for poor people. Strategies for achieving the international development targets. London: Department for International Development.

Donnelly, J. (1985) *The Concept of Human Rights*. London: Routledge.

Donnelly, J. (1999) 'Human rights, democracy and development', *Human Rights Quarterly* 21(3): 608–632.

Eccher, C. and Hornes, L. (2002) II Concurso Latinoamericano: así se hace. Ocho emprendimientos exitosos liderados por mujeres, REPEM – Red de Educacion Popular Entre Mujeres de America Latina y el Caribe. www.repem.org.uy/Txt_Asisehace_dos.htm

Edwards, M. and Hulme, D. (Eds) (1992) *Making a Difference: NGOs and development in a changing world*. London, Earthscan.

Edwards, M. and Hulme, D. (Eds) (1995) *Non-governmental Organisations – Performance and Accountability: beyond the magic bullet*. London: Save the Children and Earthscan.

Esteva, G. and Prakash, M.S. (1998) *Grassroots Postmodernism: remaking the soil of cultures*. London: Zed Books.

Evans, T. (2000) 'Citizenship and human rights in the age of globalisation', *Alternatives* 25(4): 415–438.

Ferguson, C. (1999) *Global Social Policy Principles: human rights and social justice*. London: Department for International Development.

Ferguson, J. (1990) *The Anti-Politics Machine. 'Development', depoliticisation and bureaucratic power in Lesotho*. Cambridge: Cambridge University Press.

Feuerstein, M.-T. (1986) *Partners in Evaluation*. London: Macmillan.

Flora Tristan (1995) Plan Estrategico Institucional, internal document, Lima.

Fowler, A. (2000) 'Beyond partnership. Getting real about NGO relationships in the aid system', *IDS Bulletin* 31(3): 1–13.

Fraser, A.S. (1999) 'Becoming human: the origins and development of women's human rights', *Human Rights Quarterly* 21(3): 853–906.

Freeman, M. (1995) 'Are there collective human rights?', *Political Studies* XLIII: 25–40.

Gledhill, J. (1997) Languages of rights and struggles for moral relations. Exploring the paradoxes of popular protest in Mexico. Electronic publication from the Social Anthropology website of the University of Manchester, England. www.les1.man.ac.uk/sa/jg/jgepubs.htm

Gledhill, J. (2001) 'Rights and the poor', paper presented at the ASA conference 'Anthropological perspectives on rights, claims and entitlements', University of Sussex.

Goetz, A.M. (1991) Feminism and the claim to know: contradictions in feminist approaches to women and development, in Grant, R. and Newland, K. (Eds) *Gender and International Relations*. Milton Keynes: Open University Press, pp.133–157.

González , V. and Kampwirth, K. (Eds) (2001) *Radical Women in Latin America: left and right*. University Park, PA: The Pennsylvania State University Press.

Gosling, L. and Edwards. M. (1995) *Toolkits: a practical guide to assessment, monitoring and evaluation*. London: Save the Children.

Gray Molina, G. (2001) Exclusion, participation and democratic state-building, in Crabtree, J. and Whitehead, L. (Eds) *Towards Democratic Viability: the Bolivian experience*. Houndmills: Palgrave.

Green, M. (2001) 'How "development" gets global. Making policy realities through planning practices in non-places', paper presented at the ASA conference 'Anthropological perspectives on rights, claims and entitlements', University of Sussex.

Grindle, J. (1992) *Bread and Freedom: basic human needs and human rights*, Dublin, Trócaire World Topics.

Hastrup, K. (2001) 'Representing the common good: the limits of legal language', paper presented at the ASA conference 'Anthropological perspectives on rights, claims and entitlements', University of Sussex.

Hausermann, J. (1998) *A Human Rights Based Approach to Development*. London: Rights and Humanity.

Hobart, M. (1993) *An Anthropological Critique of Development. The growth of ignorance*. London: Routledge.

Hola, E. and Portugal, A.M. (Eds) (1997) *La Ciudadanía A Debate*. Santiago: ISIS/CEM.

Huq, S.P. (2000) 'Gender and citizenship. What does a rights framework offer women?, *IDS Bulletin* 31(4): 74–82.

ICRC (2001) Quarterly Donor Report: Latin America, April–June, International Committee of the Red Cross.

Isis International Documentation and Information Center (1998) Citizens' rights are women's rights; www.undp.org/rblac/gender/citizensrights.htm

Jaquette, J.S. and Wolchik, S.L. (1998) *Women and Democracy. Latin America and Central and Eastern Europe*. Baltimore, MD: The Johns Hopkins University Press.

Jelin, E. and Hershberg, E. (1996) *Constructing Democracy: Human rights, citizenship, and society in Latin America*. Oxford: Westview Press.

Lagarde, M. (1998) *Memoria: claves feministas para el poderío y la autonomía de las mujeres*. Managua: Puntos de Encuentro.

Lagarde, M. (2000) *Memoria: claves feministas para liderazgos entrañables*. Managua: Puntos de Encuentro.

León, R. and Stahr, M. (1995) *Yo actuaba como varon solamente . . . Entrevistas a procesados por delito de violacion*. Lima: DEMUS.

López Jiménez, S. (1997) *Ciudadanos Reales e Imaginarios. Concepciones, desarrollo y mapas de la ciudadanía en el Perú*. Lima: Instituto de Dialogo y Propuestas.

Macdonald, L. (1997) *Supporting Civil Society: the political role of NGOs in Central America*. Basingstoke, Macmillan.

Mansfield, D. (1997) Evaluation: tried & tested? A review of Save the Children Evaluation reports. Working paper number 17. London: Save the Children.

Marsden, D. and Oakley, P. (Eds) (1990) *Evaluating Social Development Projects*. Oxford: Oxfam.

Merry, S.E. (2001). Changing rights, changing culture, in Cowan, J.K., Dembour, M.B. and Wilson, R. (Eds) *Culture and Rights: anthropological perspectives*. Cambridge: Cambridge University Press, pp.31–55.

Mohanty, C. (1991a) Cartographies of struggle: Third World women and the politics of feminism, in Mohanty, C., Russo, A. and Torres, L. (Eds) *Third World Women and the Politics of Feminism*. Bloomington: Indiana University Press, pp.1–50.

Mohanty, C. (1991b) Under Western eyes: feminist scholarship and colonial discourses, in Mohanty, C., Russo, A. and Torres, L. (Eds) *Third World Women and the Politics of Feminism*. Bloomington: Indiana University Press, pp.51–80.

Molyneux, M. (1985) 'Mobilization without emancipation? Women's interests, the state and revolution in Nicaragua', *Feminist Studies* 11: 227–254.

Molyneux, M. (1998) Analysing women's movements, in Jackson, C. and Pearson, R. (Eds) *Feminist Visions of Development*. London: Routledge.

Molyneux, M. (2000a) Twentieth century state formations in Latin America, in Dore, E. and Molyneux M. (Eds) *Hidden Histories of Gender and the State in Latin America*. Durham and London: Duke University Press.

Molyneux, M. (2000b) *Women's movements in international perspective: Latin America and beyond*. Houndmills: Palgrave. Reprinted in 2003 by the Institute of Latin American Studies, London.

Molyneux, M. and Razavi, S. (Eds) (2002) *Gender Justice, Development and Rights, Oxford studies in democratization*. Oxford: Oxford University Press.

Moser, C., Norton, A. with Conway, T., Ferguson, C. and Vizard, P. (2001) To claim our rights: livelihood security, human rights and sustainable development, concept paper, Workshop on Human Rights, Assets and Livelihood Security, and Sustainable Development, 19–20 June, London. www.odi.org.uk/pppg/june_workshop.html

Nelson, N. and Wright, S. (1995) *Power and Participatory Development. Theory and practice*. London: ITDG Publishing.

Normand, R. (2001) 'Letters', *The Economist* 8–14 September.

O'Donnell, G. (1996) Illusions about Consolidation, in *Journal of Democracy 7. The State in Latin America*. Durham and London: Duke University Press.

Palacios, M.A. (1997) *De que educacion ciudadana hablamos?* Lima: Tarea.

Perez Nasser, E. (1999) El Proceso de Empoderamiento de Mujeres Indígenas Organizadas desde una perspectiva de Género, Xochimilco, Mexico, Universidad Autónoma Metropolitana.

Perry, R.W. (1996) 'Rethinking the right to development: after the critique of development, after the critique of rights', *Law and Policy* 18: 225–249.

Petchesky, R.P. (2000) 'Human rights, reproductive health and economic justice: why they are indivisible', *Reproductive Health Matters* 8(15): 12–17.

Preis, A.-B. (1996) 'Human rights as cultural practice: an anthropological critique', *Human Rights Quarterly* 18: 286–315.

Rahman, M.A. (1993) *People's Self Development. Perspectives on participatory action research. A journey through experience.* London: Zed Books.

Ramos, A. (1998) *Indigenism: ethnic politics in Brazil.* Madison, London: University of Wisconsin Press.

Roberts, B.R. (1995) *The Making of Citizens: cities of peasants revisited.* London: Arnold.

Robles, C.A.M. and Ordoñez, B.D. (1996). *Perfil de las dirigentas populares: Capacitación y liderazgo.* Lima: FOVIDA.

Roos, J. (2001) 'Using socio-economic rights in post-Apartheid South Africa', paper presented at the 'Workshop on human rights, assets and livelihood security, and sustainable development', 19–20 June, Overseas Development Institute, London.

Rowlands, J. (1998) A word of the times, but what does it mean? Empowerment in the discourse and practice of development, in Afshar, H. (Ed.) *Women and Empowerment.* New York: St Martins Press.

Rozga, D. (2001) 'Applying a human rights based approach to programming: experiences of UNICEF', paper presented at the 'Workshop on human rights, assets and livelihood security, and sustainable development', 19–20 June, Overseas Development Institute, London.

Sano, H.-O. (2000) 'Development and human rights: the necessary, but partial integration of human rights and development', *Human Rights Quarterly* 22(3): 734–752.

Scott, C. (1999) 'Reaching beyond (without abandoning) the category of "economic, social and cultural rights"', *Human Rights Quarterly* 21(3): 633–660.

Scott, J.C. (1998) *Seeing Like A State.* New Haven, Connecticut and London: Yale University Press.

Scott, J.W. (1996) *Only Paradoxes to Offer. French feminists and the rights of man.* Cambridge, MA: Harvard University Press.

Sen, A. (1992) *Inequality Reexamined.* Oxford: Oxford University Press.

Sieder, R. (2002) Introduction, in Sieder, R. (Ed.) *Multiculturalism in Latin America: indigenous rights, diversity and democracy.* Houndmills, Palgrave, pp.1–23.

Stammers, N. (1999) 'Social movements and the social construction of human rights', *Human Rights Quarterly* 21(4): 980–1008.

Stavenhagen, R. (2002) Indigenous peoples and the state in Latin America: an ongoing debate, in Sieder, R. (Ed.) *Multiculturalism in Latin America: indigenous rights, diversity and democracy.* Houndmills, Palgrave, pp.24–44.

Streeten, P. et al. (1981) *First Things First. Meeting basic human needs in developing countries.* New York: OUP/World Bank.

Stromquist, N. (2002) Education as a means for empowering women, in Parpart, J.L., Rai, S. and Staudt, K. (Eds) *Rethinking Empowerment: gender and development in a global/local world.* London: Routledge.

Subrahmanian, R. (2002) Engendering education: prospects for a rights-based approach to female education deprivation in India, in Molyneux, M. and Razavi, S. (Eds) *Gender Justice Development and Rights.* Oxford: Oxford University Press.

Tang, K.-L. (2000) 'The leadership role of international law in enforcing women's rights: the optional protocol to the Women's Convention', *Gender and Development* 8(3): 65–73.

The Economist (2001) 'Human Rights. Righting Wrongs', *The Economist*, 18 August.

Townsend, J., Zapata, E., Rolands, J., Alberti, P. and Mercado, M. (Eds) (1999) *Women and Power: fighting patriarchies and poverty.* London and New York: Zed Books.

UNDP (2000) *Human Development Report 2000 – Human Rights and Human Development.* http://hdr.undp.org/reports/global/2000/en/

UNDP (2002) *Human Development Report 2002 – Deepening Democracy in a Fragmented World.* www.undp.org/hdr2002

UNIFEM (2002) Ending Violence Against Women Around the World, press release 7 August: www.unifem.undp.org

United Nations (2001) Substantive issues arising in the implementation of the International Covenant on Economic, Social and Cultural Rights: Poverty and the International Covenant on Economic, Social and Cultural Rights, statement adopted by the Committee of the Economic and Social Council, E/C 12/2001/10. Geneva: UN.

Urioste, M. (2001) *Bolivia. Reform and Resistance in the Countryside (1982–2000).* London: Institute of Latin American Studies.

Van Cott, D.L. (1994) *Indigenous Peoples and Democracy in Latin America.* New York: St Martin's Press.

Van Cott, D.L. (2000) *The Friendly Liquidation of the Past. The politics of diversity in Latin America.* Pittsburgh, PA: University of Pittsburgh Press.

van Weerelt, P. (2001) 'A rights-based approach to development programming in UNDP: adding the missing link', paper presented at the 'Workshop on human rights, assets and livelihood security, and sustainable development', 19–20 June, Overseas Development Institute, London.

Whitehead, A. (2001) 'Policy discourses on women's land rights in sub-Saharan Africa: the return to 'customary law' and the prospects for achieving gender justice', paper presented at the ASA conference 'Anthropological perspectives on rights, claims and entitlements', University of Sussex, Brighton.

Wilson, R. (Ed.) (1997) *Human Rights, Culture and Context: anthropological perspectives*. London: Pluto Press.

Wollstonecraft, M. (1975 [1792]). *A Vindication of the Rights of Woman*. London: Penguin.

World Bank (1998) *Development and Human Rights: the role of the World Bank*. Washington, DC: World Bank.

World Bank (2001) *World Development Report 2000/2001: attacking poverty*. Washington, DC: World Bank.

Yanni, V.F.K. (1997) *Health Reviews. Not re-inventing the wheel: learning from evaluations of Oxfam involvement in health (1987–1997)*. Oxford: Oxfam.

Index